Cordon Bleu

Casseroles

Cordon Bleu

Casseroles

(Casserole cooking and braising)

Macdonald and Jane's
London

Published by
Macdonald and Jane's Publishers Ltd
Paulton House
8 Shepherdess Walk
London N1

This impression 1977

Designed by Melvin Kyte
Printed by Waterlow (Dunstable) Ltd

These recipes have been adapted from the Cordon Bleu Cookery Course published by Purnell in association with the London Cordon Bleu Cookery School

Principal: Rosemary Hume; Co-Principal: Muriel Downes

Quantities given are for 4 servings.

Spoon measures are level unless otherwise stated.

Contents

Introduction

Lift off the lid, and out pours a delicious blend of savoury smells. Some form of hot pot is among the national dishes of practically every European country, and there are many from North America too. These one-dish meals have a universal appeal which springs, probably, from the idea of a multitude of good things crowded into one serving pot.

Casserole cooking and braising are two forms of economical hot pot cooking that produce the most delicious results. Neither demands the best cuts of meat, or the finest vegetables. Slow, gentle cooking helps to make even tough cuts tenderer, and every drop of juice from meat or vegetables will be served in the finished dish, to make it as nourishing as it is full-flavoured. All kinds of meat, poultry, game, or vegetable can be cooked in a braise or casserole and the resulting dish will be tender and succulent, in rich, strong gravy or sauce.

For family meals and party cooking, both casseroles and braises have other advantages than economy. It is usually possible to prepare the dish early in the day and leave it in the oven to finish cooking with very little attention needed at the last minute. It can also be left in the oven after cooking is complete without spoiling — an advantage that mothers with unpunctual families, or hosts with delayed guests, will fully appreciate !

In the appendix to this book we have included a glossary of some of the special cooking terms used and notes on the preparation of various items that recur throughout the book. Experienced cooks may not need to use this, but if there is anything you do not understand in a recipe you will probably find it further explained in the appendix.

Rosemary Hume
Muriel Downes

7

Meat dishes

Cheaper cuts of meat are often tasty, but tough. Fast cooking, such as roasting or grilling, dries them out and hardens them still further. For these, try casserole cooking, in which the meat is cut in pieces and cooked slowly, in a covered pot, in a liquid or sauce that keeps the meat tender and juicy. Add other ingredients, such as mushrooms and tomatoes, to give an extra flavour and richness to the sauce.

A casserole is the joy of the busy cook as it can be served in the dish in which it is cooked — straight from oven to table.

Today there are many types of flameproof casserole on the market so that the ingredients can also be browned conveniently on top of the stove in the same dish, before transferring to the oven for slow cooking.

For slightly better cuts of meat, that are still tough but which can be left whole, braising is the answer. Again cooking is done in a pot, with a tight fitting lid, in the oven so that the dish has both top and bottom heat. For a good braise, though, it is essential to use a very small quantity of liquid ; the food cooks in the steam from the liquid, keeping moist that way.

Choosing the right pan is important ; it should be of enamelled iron, cast iron or thick aluminium and be deep enough for the chosen joint to fit snugly into it. Glass, or any other non-flameproof ovenware, however, is not suitable for braises as part of the cooking is done on top of the stove.

For meat dishes cooked in either of these ways, start by browning the meat all over in hot fat. Then, for casseroles, add any other solid ingredients to the pan, continue to fry for a moment or two, then add stock and seasoning according to the recipe. Cook in a very slow oven until the meat is thoroughly tender.

For braises, take the meat out of the pan when it is brown and put in a good plateful of sliced or diced vegetables (onion, carrot, a little turnip and celery).

This is called a mirepoix and is used for flavouring and to lift the meat from the base of the pan so that it does not overcook. Cover the pan and cook gently for 5-7 minutes. This allows the vegetables to absorb excess fat and to take colour. Put back the meat on top of the mirepoix, together with a bouquet garni and a little seasoning. Pour in a little liquid, as required by the recipe, and cover the pan closely. Baste and turn the meat during cooking. A sauce is made with the gravy from the pan, and the vegetables are discarded after cooking as their job of flavouring is now done and they will be overcooked.

Normally you would cook a braising joint for 1-2 hours (depending on size) in a slow oven at 325°F or Mark 3. If, however, you choose to braise a roasting joint, less time can be allowed (20 minutes per lb and 20 minutes over).

For a really successful braise it is essential to have a slightly jellied brown stock. If the stock is not strong, tuck a pig's trotter in beside the joint, — this gives a beautifully sticky finish to the sauce.

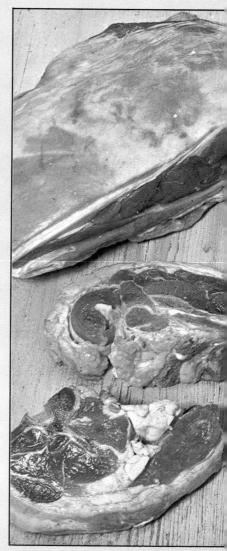

Economical cuts of lamb : (from left to right, top) half shoulder, double scrag, gigot ; (below) chump chops and loin chops

Lamb and tomato casserole

1½- 2 lb middle neck of lamb
salt and pepper
paprika pepper
1 oz butter
2 onions (thinly sliced)
2 cups tomatoes (14 oz can),
    or 1 lb fresh tomatoes and
    1 teaspoon tomato purée (optional)
2-3 tablespoons soured cream, or
    yoghourt
1 tablespoon chopped parsley

Method
Set oven at 275°F or Mark 1. Divide meat into neat pieces, rub with seasoning. Heat butter on top of stove in flameproof casserole and brown meat on both sides. Take out meat, add onions and allow to brown. Replace meat in casserole, add tomatoes. If using fresh tomatoes, skin, squeeze to remove seeds, slice and cook to a pulp before adding them. A teaspoon of tomato purée can also be added to fresh tomatoes to strengthen flavour.

Cover tightly, cook slowly until meat is very tender (1-1½ hours) in pre-set oven. (Cooking on top of stove may result in over-reduction of liquid.)

If using an earthenware casserole, first brown meat in a pan, then pack into casserole.

Add a little stock during cooking, if necessary, but gravy should be concentrated and well-reduced. Before serving, add cream to juices in casserole and spoon over meat. Sprinkle with parsley. Serve creamed potatoes (page 30) and onion ragoût (page 70).

Lamb chops with aubergines

4 lamb chops, or 2 large gigot chops
4 tablespoons oil
2 oz butter
4 onions (sliced)
2 medium-size aubergines (sliced
    and lightly salted)
salt and pepper
1 clove of garlic (crushed)
2 teaspoons tomato purée
2 wineglasses stock (see page 134)
6-8 tomatoes (skinned, sliced and
    seeds removed)
4 tablespoons grated cheese
2 tablespoons chopped parsley

Gigot chops are a Scots joint and are cut from the top of the leg. One large gigot chop is enough for two people and can be used for a sauté or braise.

Method
Set the oven at 350°F or Mark 4. Heat the oil and butter and fry the lamb chops quickly on both sides to brown them well. Then remove chops from pan.

Reheat frying pan, add a little more oil if necessary and fry the onions until turning brown. Take them out and put in the drained aubergine slices and fry for 5-6 minutes, turning frequently. Replace the onions and season, add garlic, tomato purée, stock and tomatoes. Bring to the boil. Turn half of this into an ovenproof casserole (or flameproof one if using the top of the stove), place chops on top and cover with rest of the aubergine and tomato mixture. Dust the top with grated cheese, and put dish uncovered into the pre-set moderate oven (or cook covered on top of the stove) for about 35-40 minutes. Dust the top thickly with parsley and serve hot with potatoes.

American lamb hot pot

1 large leg of lamb, or 2 small ones
(the joints must be large enough
to give 3 lb meat when cut from
the bone)
4 tablespoons plain flour (sifted
with 1 teaspoon salt and $\frac{1}{2}$ teaspoon
pepper)
2 tablespoons dripping
4 large onions (finely chopped)
4 tablespoons tomato purée
4 pints jellied stock (see page 134)
$\frac{1}{2}$ lb mushrooms
3-4 lb large potatoes
2 oz butter
grated Parmesan cheese (for
dusting)

This dish serves 12 people and
is suitable for a lunch party.
We have therefore given instructions for preparing part of
the dish the day before to save
time on the day of the party.

Method

Cut the meat from the bone into
1-1$\frac{1}{2}$ inch cubes. (Perhaps the
butcher will do this ; if so,
remember to ask him for the
bone, from which you can make
your stock.) Set the oven at
325°F or Mark 3.

Roll the meat in the sifted
flour, heat the dripping in a
large flameproof casserole and,
when hot, fry the meat until
well sealed and golden-brown
on all sides.

Watchpoint Do not put in more
meat than would cover the
bottom of the casserole at once ;
for this quantity you will have
to fry the meat in rotation.

When all the meat is well
coloured, add the finely
chopped onions to the pan,
cover and lower the heat. Leave
to cook until the onion has lost
its hard white look and is well
softened. Shake the pan and

stir from time to time. Work in
the tomato purée and the stock
and bring to the boil. Add a
little extra salt and pepper if
necessary, then cover the pan
tightly and cook in the pre-set
oven for 1$\frac{1}{2}$-2 hours.

Meanwhile, wash, trim and
quarter mushrooms, add them
to hot pot at end of cooking
time and return to oven for
another 10-15 minutes.

Prepare as far as this the day
before the party and turn into a
large mixing bowl to allow the
meat to cool quickly, or into
open casseroles, or gratin
dishes, ready for reheating.

The following day scrub the
potatoes and steam, or boil, in
their skins until tender. Peel
while still hot, holding each
potato in a tea cloth to prevent
burning fingers, and cut into
$\frac{1}{2}$-inch slices. Arrange these overlapping to form a cover to the
meat. Brush the potatoes with
melted butter, dust with a very
little Parmesan cheese and bake
in a pre-set oven, at 375°F or
Mark 5, for 30 minutes, until the
potatoes are crusty and brown.

Breast of lamb Fallette

2 small lean breasts of lamb
  (about 2 lb in all)
1 large onion (for braising)
2 carrots (for braising)
2 sticks of celery (for braising)
3-4 bacon rashers
bouquet garni
$\frac{1}{2}$ pint jellied bone stock (see page
  134)
chopped parsley

For stuffing
2 lambs kidneys
6 oz cooked ham (shoulder cut)
$\frac{1}{2}$ clove of garlic
2 oz white breadcrumbs
1 large handful of spinach leaves
  (about 5 oz)
1 small egg
salt and pepper

For brown sauce
2 shallots
1 oz butter
$\frac{3}{4}$ oz plain flour
1 rounded teaspoon tomato purée
$\frac{3}{4}$ pint brown stock (see page 134)
bouquet garni

Method

Bone out the breasts of lamb and split them carefully at the side to form a pocket in each one.

Set oven at 350°F or Mark 4.

Dice the braising vegetables, line the bottom of a deep flame-proof pan or casserole with the bacon rashers and place the vegetables on these. Cover pan and set it on a low heat to sweat the vegetables.

To prepare stuffing : skin and core kidney and chop with the ham and garlic. Stir in the breadcrumbs, then finely chop the spinach and add with the egg to the mixture. Season well. Fill stuffing into the pockets in the breasts, taking care not to stuff them too tightly, then sew up with fine string.

Set breasts on the braising vegetables, add bouquet garni and pour around the stock. Put lamb to cook (uncovered) in pre-set oven, for about 1-1$\frac{1}{2}$ hours,

Splitting the breasts at the sides

Sewing up stuffed breasts with string

basting it occasionally.

Meanwhile prepare brown sauce : chop the shallots finely and soften them in half the butter ; add the remaining butter, blend in the flour and allow it to brown slowly. Draw pan aside, add tomato purée and stock. Bring sauce to boil, add bouquet garni, season lightly and simmer, uncovered, for 20-25 minutes, skimming it if necessary. Then strain sauce.

When the meat is tender and brown, lift out of pan or casserole, remove the string and dish up. Coat it with a little of the sauce and dust thickly with chopped parsley. Serve the rest of the sauce in a sauce boat, and accompany with creamed potatoes (see page 30).

Armenian lamb with pilaf

2 lb fillet end of leg of lamb
1 tablespoon oil
1 oz butter
2 medium-size onions (sliced)
1 clove of garlic (chopped)
1 tablespoon plain flour
1 teaspoon ground cumin seed
$\frac{1}{2}$ teaspoon ground allspice
2 tablespoons tomato purée
$\frac{1}{2}$-$\frac{3}{4}$ pint stock (see page 134)
salt and pepper

Method

Cut the meat from the bone and divide into 2-inch squares. Heat the oil in a sauté pan, or deep flameproof casserole, drop in the butter and, when foaming, brown the meat a few pieces at a time.

Remove the meat, add the onions and garlic and cook slowly for 5 minutes, stirring from time to time ; dust in the flour and spices and continue cooking a further 3-4 minutes. Stir in the tomato purée and $\frac{1}{2}$ pint of stock, away from the

Heat the oil in a sauté pan or deep casserole and add the butter. When the butter is foaming, drop in a few pieces of lamb at a time and cook each piece until brown

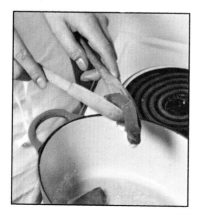

heat, and blend until mixture is smooth.

Return pan to the stove and stir mixture until boiling ; reduce the heat, add the meat to pan, cover and cook for 45-60 minutes on top of the stove or in the oven at 350°F or Mark 4. Stir the mixture occasionally, adding the reserved stock, if necessary, and season to taste.

Dish up the meat on a serving dish, piling it up neatly. Reduce the gravy to a thick sauce, if necessary, and spoon it over. There should be sufficient to moisten it. Arrange pilaf at each end of the dish or serve it separately. Serve a green salad in season.

Pilaf

1$\frac{1}{2}$ oz butter
1 small onion (finely chopped)
8$\frac{1}{2}$ oz long grain rice
$\frac{3}{4}$ pint chicken stock (see page 134)
salt and pepper
3 oz currants (washed)
3 oz pistachio nuts (blanched and shredded — see page 137)

Method

Melt two-thirds of the butter in a flameproof casserole, add the onion and cook slowly until just golden-brown ; stir in the rice and continue cooking for 2-3 minutes. Pour on the stock, season and bring it to the boil. Cover the casserole and cook in the oven at 375°F or Mark 5 until the rice is tender (about 20 minutes).

Add extra stock to moisten, if necessary, and put the rest of the butter in casserole, with the currants and pistachio nuts, forking them in very carefully.

Lamb goulash

6 lamb chump ends
2 rounded tablespoons dripping
2 large onions (preferably Spanish)
  — finely sliced
2 dessertspoons paprika pepper
2 dessertspoons plain flour
1 clove of garlic (crushed)
  — optional
2 dessertspoons tomato purée
1 pint stock (see page 134), or water
1 bayleaf
2 large tomatoes (skinned, sliced
  and seeds removed)
salt and pepper
4 tablespoons yoghourt
2 tablespoons chopped parsley

Chump ends are cut from the tail end of the loin and, because they have a fairly large proportion of bone, are sold quite cheaply. Braise rather than grill them, and use for making goulash or stews (cooked in the oven or on top of the stove). They can be cooked in the same way as oxtail.

Method
If using the oven, set it at 350°F or Mark 4. Wipe the meat. Heat a stewpan or flameproof casserole, put in dripping and when hot add the meat. Brown for about 4-5 minutes, then add the onion and continue to fry gently for a further 5 minutes. Add paprika, mix well. Cook for 2-3 seconds then draw aside and stir in the flour and add garlic, tomato purée, stock or water, and bayleaf.

Bring slowly to the boil, cover and cook on top of the stove, or in the pre-set moderate oven, for about 50 minutes until tender, and then add the tomato. Adjust seasoning, take out bayleaf and spoon over the yoghourt and dust thickly with chopped parsley. Serve with noodles or plainly boiled potatoes.

Alternatively, if using oven for goulash, serve boulangère potatoes (see page 137).

Savoury stuffed loin of lamb

3 lb loin of lamb (boned)
salt and pepper
pinch of dried marjoram
2 oz butter
2 large carrots (cut in rounds)
3 medium-size onions (peeled)
bouquet garni
1 wineglass white wine
6 oz mushrooms
4 tablespoons dried white breadcrumbs (see page 136)
2 tablespoons grated Parmesan
cheese

Method

Season the boned surface of the lamb with salt, pepper and marjoram, tie joint securely with string or fasten with poultry pins. Drop 1 oz butter in a deep cocotte (cast iron casserole), put in the meat, cook quickly for 4-5 minutes on all sides (just enough to seal the meat). Reduce the heat, add the carrots, whole onions, bouquet garni, and season. Pour over the wine and cover cocotte tightly. Cook very slowly for 1 hour.

Trim and wash mushrooms, chop them finely and cook in remaining butter until all the moisture has evaporated ; rub them through a sieve.

When cooked, remove the onions from the cocotte with a draining spoon, rub them through a strainer, mix with the mushroom purée and season well. Then set the oven at 375°F or Mark 5.

Take up the meat, which should still be pink in the centre, and carve in thick slices. Spread the purée between the slices and reshape joint in an oven-proof gratin dish, holding the meat in shape by running two skewers through the slices, one from each end. Mix the bread-crumbs and cheese together, sprinkle over the meat and season again. Brown joint lightly in pre-set moderate oven for about 20-30 minutes. Strain the juices left in the cocotte and pour them over the meat before serving.

Braised stuffed leg of lamb

1 small leg of lamb (about 3½ lb)
8 anchovy fillets
3 tablespoons milk (for soaking anchovy)
8 oz cooked gammon (sliced)
1 shallot (finely chopped)
1 teaspoon chopped parsley
pinch of chopped thyme, or marjoram

For braising
2 carrots (diced)
2 onions (diced)
2-3 sticks of celery (diced)
1-2 tablespoons oil
2 cloves of garlic
1 wineglass red wine (optional)
½ pint jellied brown bone stock (see page 134)
bouquet garni

For sauce
1 oz butter
2 shallots (finely chopped)
1 tablespoon plain flour
1 large teaspoon tomato purée
¾ pint jellied bone stock (page 134)

Method

Ask your butcher to bone the leg of lamb without cutting the skin. Soak half the anchovies in a little milk to remove excess salt. Lay the gammon slices overlapping on a board, drain the anchovy fillets and place on top. Sprinkle well with the shallot and herbs and roll up to form a tube. Push this into boned lamb and tie up securely.

Lard the meat with the remaining anchovies, ie. sew them into the meat with a larding needle.

Set the oven at 350°F or Mark 4. Heat the oil in a heavy cocotte, brown the meat lightly on all sides, then take out of the pan. Add the diced vegetables,

To stuff the boned leg of lamb, first place anchovy fillets on gammon slices, sprinkle with chopped shallot and herbs. Roll up into a tube, open up meat and stuff in the gammon

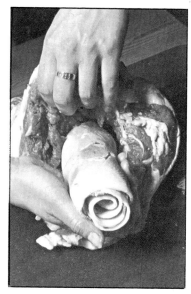

cover pan and reduce heat to cook gently for 8-10 minutes until they have taken colour and absorbed the fat. Place the leg of lamb on the vegetables, add the garlic. Add the wine and flame it (heat and set it alight to burn out alcohol), then the stock ; tuck the bouquet garni alongside and bring to the boil. Cover the pan and cook meat in the pre-set oven for 2 hours.

To prepare the sauce : melt the butter in a pan, add the shallot, cook slowly until soft, then stir in the flour and brown slowly. Stir in the tomato purée and stock, bring to the boil and simmer for 30-40 minutes.

Take cooked meat from oven, strain off the liquid and boil to reduce to half the quantity. Add this to the sauce.

Remove the strings from the meat, place it on a serving dish and pour over a little of the sauce. Pour the rest into a sauceboat and serve separately.

Leg of lamb bretonne

$3\frac{1}{2}$-4 lb leg of lamb
8 oz tomatoes
1 clove of garlic
salt and pepper
1 tablespoon dripping
1 wineglass white wine, or stock (see page 134)
1 bayleaf

Method

Set the oven at 325°F or Mark 3. Scald and skin the tomatoes, remove the seeds and chop flesh finely. Crush the garlic with $\frac{1}{2}$ teaspoon salt.

Brown the meat on all sides in hot dripping in a heavy flame-proof pan. Place the tomatoes and garlic round meat, season with pepper and pour over the white wine or stock. Add the bayleaf, cover the pan and braise for about 2 hours in the pre-set oven.

Adjust seasoning and add extra wine or stock, if the sauce is too thick.

Serve with haricot beans with cream sauce (see page 22); these are a good accompaniment to lamb or mutton.

Haricot beans
with cream sauce

4 oz dried haricot beans
1 teaspoon bicarbonate of soda
  to 2 quarts boiling water (for
  soaking)
1 head of celery (sliced)
8 oz button onions
1 tablespoon chopped parsley

For $\frac{3}{4}$ pint cream sauce
1 $\frac{1}{2}$ oz butter
1 $\frac{1}{2}$ oz plain flour
$\frac{3}{4}$ pint milk
salt and pepper
2-3 tablespoons single cream

Method
Wash the beans in several
changes of water. Pour on the
boiling water (with bicarbonate
of soda) and leave beans to
soak overnight. After soaking,
rinse the beans well and place
in a pan with celery and whole
onions. Cover with cold water
and bring very slowly to the
boil. Simmer gently for about
1 hour until beans are tender.

To prepare the sauce ; make
a roux with the butter and flour,
add liquid off heat, season well
and add the cream. Return to
heat and boil.

Drain the vegetables and add
to the sauce with the chopped
parsley. Turn into a casserole
for serving with lamb or mutton
dishes.

Biriani

2 lb leg of lamb
4 green chillies (seeded)
1 clove of garlic (crushed with salt)
2-3 sprays of coriander, or mint,
  leaves
2 teaspoons cumin powder
1 teaspoon chilli powder
1 teaspoon garam masala
1 carton (5 fl oz) plain yoghourt
4 medium-size onions (thinly sliced)
5 $\frac{1}{2}$ oz butter
$\frac{3}{4}$ pint water
1 dessertspoon salt
1 lb potatoes (boiled and
  quartered)
pinch of saffron
$\frac{1}{3}$ pint hot milk
1 lb long grain Busmatti, or
  Patna, rice
1 $\frac{1}{2}$ oz shredded almonds
  (unblanched)
2 oz sultanas (washed)

For salad
2 onions (chopped)
4 tomatoes (chopped)
2 green chillies (seeded and
  finely chopped)
sugar
salt
vinegar

Method
Remove the meat from the bone
and cut off some of the fat.
Cut the meat into 2-inch
squares. Chop the chillies very
finely, then mix them with the
garlic, coriander and spices and
add the yoghourt. Add the
diced meat to yoghourt mixture.
Mix well and marinate for 1 hour.

Fry the onions in 4 oz butter
until brown. Remove from the
pan, add the meat to the pan
and fry for about 5 minutes,
turning it well so that it does
not stick to the pan. Add $\frac{3}{4}$ pint
of water and 1 dessertspoon of

salt, cover and cook gently. When the meat is almost tender (about 45-50 minutes), add the potatoes and add more salt if necessary.

Leave the saffron to infuse in the hot milk for 10 minutes. Put the rice into boiling salted water and boil for 10 minutes, or until barely cooked, then drain. When the meat is tender, remove it with its sauce, reduce if necessary, mix with half the onions and a quarter of the rice, moisten with 2-3 tablespoons of the saffron milk. Lay this on the bottom of an ovenproof casserole together with the potatoes. Cover the top with the remaining rice and sprinkle the rest of the saffron milk on top. Cover with dampened muslin to keep rice moist. Put on a lid and continue cooking in the oven at 350°F or Mark 4 for 30 minutes.

Meanwhile fry the almonds to a pale gold in the remaining butter, add the sultanas and fry for a minute longer to plump them.

Serve biriani with the rest of the onions sprinkled over it and the almonds and sultanas on top. Accompany with a salad of onions, tomatoes and green chillies, mixed with sugar, salt and vinegar to taste.

Serve this spicy Indian dish with a salad of onions, tomatoes and chillies

Braised spiced leg of lamb

1 small leg of lamb (about 3 lb)
2 teaspoons ground coriander
1 teaspoon cumin powder
1 teaspoon paprika pepper
1 teaspoon salt
½ teaspoon black pepper
½ teaspoon ground ginger
2 tablespoons oil
1 oz butter
1 large carrot (sliced)
1 large onion (sliced)
2 sticks of celery (sliced)
¼-½ pint good bone stock (see page 134)
bouquet garni
1 teaspoon tomato purée
kneaded butter, or arrowroot (slaked)

Method

Mix the spices together, then rub these into the leg of lamb and leave overnight, or for at least 1-2 hours.

Set oven at 325-350°F or Mark 3-4.

When ready to braise, heat the oil and butter in a large flameproof casserole, put in the lamb and allow it to brown rather slowly. Do not overcolour, or the spices may become singed and so lose their flavour. Take out the lamb, add all the vegetables, cover and sweat for 5-6 minutes. Replace the lamb and add the stock, bouquet garni and tomato purée. Cover tightly and braise in the pre-set oven for 1½-2 hours, or until the lamb is very tender.

When ready to dish up, take out the joint and strain the juices from the pot. Thicken the juices slightly with kneaded butter, or arrowroot, and reboil. Replace the lamb in the pot, pour over the gravy, cover and set aside until ready to serve. (This can be prepared in advance and left to marinate in the gravy, then reheated in the oven at 350°F or Mark 4 for 20-30 minutes.) Serve with flageolets toulousaines (opposite) and maître d'hôtel potatoes (see page 138).

To prepare the leg of lamb, spices are spooned over and rubbed in. Vegetables are sliced for braising

Right : braised spiced leg of lamb has gravy spooned over to serve

Flageolets toulousaines

1 can (about 15 oz) flageolets
1 tablespoon oil, or 1 oz butter
2 or more cloves of garlic
  (crushed with salt)
3 ripe tomatoes (scalded,
  skinned, seeds removed)
salt and pepper

In this country it is easier to buy canned than fresh flageolets. They are delicious, small green kidney beans, much used in France.

Method
Put the oil (or butter) into a pan or flameproof dish, add the garlic and tomatoes and soften to a pulp. Then add the flageolets (drained) and season. Cover and simmer for 7-10 minutes, or until all the ingredients are thoroughly mixed. Serve hot.

Drained flageolets are added to garlic-flavoured tomato pulp to make the flageolets toulousaines which accompany braised leg of lamb

Hot pot

6 mutton chops
3 large onions (thinly sliced)
4 oz flat mushrooms (quartered)
3 lambs kidneys
2 lb potatoes
dripping
salt and pepper
1 pint strong stock (see page 134)

Choose a large ovenproof casserole in which to cook and serve this good, old-fashioned and very English dish.

Method
Set oven at 350°F or Mark 4. Trim the chops, prepare the onions and mushrooms. Skin and halve the kidneys, peel and slice the potatoes.

Rub the casserole well with dripping. Arrange a good layer of the potatoes on the bottom and scatter over the onions. Arrange chops on this, season and lay the halved kidneys with the mushrooms on top. Cover with the rest of the potatoes, arranging the last layer neatly. Dot with dripping and pour in the stock at the side.

Cover and put into pre-set oven for 30 minutes. Then lower heat to 325°F or Mark 3 and leave for $1\frac{1}{2}$ hours. Then remove lid and allow potatoes to brown well. Increase heat a little during this stage and add a little extra stock if necessary.

The extra chops allow for two second helpings when serving 4 people.

Steak and kidney hot pot

$1\frac{1}{2}$ lb skirt, or shin, of beef
$\frac{1}{2}$ lb ox kidney
1 tablespoon dripping
1 rounded tablespoon plain flour
1 medium-size onion (finely chopped)
$\frac{1}{4}$ lb mushrooms (sliced)
salt and pepper
$\frac{3}{4}$ pint stock (see page 134)
1-1$\frac{1}{2}$ lb potatoes (peeled and sliced)
1-2 oz dripping, or butter

Method
Set oven at 325°F or Mark 3. Cut the meat into $\frac{1}{2}$-inch dice. Cut kidney the same size, removing the core. Brown the beef quickly in the dripping and draw aside. Roll the kidney in the flour. Pack meat, onion and kidney into a thick casserole with the mushrooms and plenty of seasoning. Pour on the stock and cover casserole with tight-fitting lid. Cook slowly on top of the stove or in the pre-set oven for 2-3 hours or until the meat is very tender.

After the first hour, cover the top with a thick layer of potatoes, dot with dripping (or butter), cover again and continue cooking. Remove lid a good 30 minutes before the meat is cooked to allow the potatoes to become crusty.

Boeuf à la mode

3-4 lb top rump, or aitchbone, of beef
1-2 tablespoons dripping
½ pint white, or red, wine
water, or bone stock (see page 134) to cover
1 calf's foot (split)
2 oz rasher of green streaky bacon, or pickled pork
4 medium-size carrots
3 medium-size onions
bouquet garni
½ teaspoon salt
6 peppercorns

This is made with a good-sized piece of top rump never less than 3 lb in weight, preferably larger, as the success of the dish depends on very long and slow cooking. Top rump is the best cut to choose for this dish as it has a piece of natural fat along the side which will help to keep the meat moist and succulent throughout the long cooking : this is preferable to topside, which usually has added fat tied to the joint. A cut from the aitchbone would also be good. Flavour is imparted to the meat by onions, carrots and wine, and the true texture of the gravy can only be produced by the addition of a calf's foot.

If the meat is to be served hot, extra carrots and onions are cooked separately (and are added after the meat is sliced and the gravy strained over) as the original flavouring vegetables would be over-cooked and tasteless by the time the meat is tender.

Method

Set oven at 275°F or Mark 1.

Heat a heavy flameproof casserole, put in the dripping and brown the meat thoroughly on all sides, then drain off the fat, moisten meat with the wine and simmer gently to reduce wine to half quantity. Add stock (or water) to come level with the beef and bring to the boil.

Meanwhile wash the calf's foot very well, cover with cold water and boil for 5 minutes ; drain and refresh. Cut the bacon or pork into lardons and blanch in the same way. Add the vegetables, bouquet garni, calf's foot, bacon, salt and peppercorns to the casserole containing the beef and bring to the boil. Skim well, then cover the pan with a tightly fitting lid and cook very gently in a slow oven for about 4 hours. During this time, turn the meat 2 or 3 times.

To serve, skim the sauce very well to remove the fat, carve the meat in fairly thick slices and arrange overlapping in a fireproof dish. Strain the sauce over the meat and, if the meat is to be served cold, leave it to set so that it becomes a jelly. If the meat is to be served hot, place freshly cooked onions and carrots in the dish, strain the sauce and spoon it over the meat.

Watchpoint The meat should be so tender and well cooked that you should be able to cut it with a spoon.

Beef and corn casserole

1½-2 lb chuck steak
2 corn cobs, or 1 small can of
   sweetcorn kernels
2-3 tablespoons dripping
2 medium-size onions (sliced)
1 tablespoon plain flour
1 rounded tablespoon tomato
   purée
¾-1 pint good stock (see page 134)
bouquet garni
salt and pepper
3-4 ripe tomatoes
chopped parsley (to garnish)

Method

Cut the meat into 1½-inch chunks and brown quickly in 2-3 tablespoons of dripping ; take out and add the sliced onions. Lower the heat and allow onions to brown. Stir in the flour and add the tomato purée, stock and bouquet garni ; season, and stir until boiling.

Replace the meat (there should be just enough gravy to cover the pieces), cover the pan and simmer gently for about 1¼

hours either on the top of cooker or in a pre-set slow to moderate oven at 325-350°F or Mark 3-4.

Meanwhile strip the husks from the corn cobs and put them into boiling water for 3-4 minutes, then drain. With a fork or sharp knife pull out, or cut down, the cobs to take away the kernels.

Watchpoint If using canned kernels, drain off the liquid. If using cobs, they should yield about 1 cup of kernels.

Take out the beef, removing the bouquet garni, and mix with the kernels. Scald and skin the tomatoes, squeeze away the seeds and slice flesh thickly Add tomatoes to the pan, return the beef and corn, cover and continue to cook until beef is very tender (about 30-40 minutes). At the end of this time the gravy should be well reduced. Adjust seasoning and serve, well sprinkled with parsley.

Braised beef flamande
with tomato coulis

2½ lb joint of topside beef
2 tablespoons dripping
plate of mixed root vegetables
   (sliced)
¼ pint brown ale
¼ pint stock (see page 134)
bouquet garni
1 teaspoon tomato purée
kneaded butter, or 1 dessertspoon arrowroot (slaked with
   1 tablespoon cold water)
chopped parsley

For tomato coulis
1 lb tomatoes (skinned, seeds
   removed and sliced)
1 Spanish onion (sliced in rings)
1 tablespoon oil, or dripping

Coulis is French for a soup stew
or liquid thickened with pieces
of vegetables or meat.

Method
Brown the joint of beef all over
in the hot dripping in a flameproof casserole. Take out the
meat, put in the prepared
vegetables, cover and sweat
them for 7 minutes. Then
replace the meat, pour round
ale and stock, add bouquet
garni and tomato purée. Cover
tightly and braise on top of the
stove for about 1½ hours or until
tender.

When beef is cooked, make
the tomato coulis by frying
onion rings until just brown
in the dripping in a frying pan.
Then add the prepared tomatoes.
Season, cover pan and cook
for 2-3 minutes only until
tomatoes are just soft.

Slice the beef, strain gravy
and thicken with kneaded butter
or arrowroot. Dish up tomatoes
and arrange slices of beef on
top, spoon over a little of the
gravy and serve the rest
separately. Dust well with
parsley.

Serve with carrots in poulette
sauce (see recipe on page 136)
and creamed potatoes (see page
30).

Carbonade of beef

1½-2 lb chuck steak
1-2 tablespoons dripping
2 onions (sliced)
1 tablespoon plain flour
1 clove of garlic
½ teaspoon salt
½ pint hot water
½ pint brown ale
bouquet garni
pepper
pinch of grated nutmeg
pinch of sugar
1 teaspoon wine vinegar

Carbonade used to mean a dish that was grilled or boiled over the coals (carbone). It now denotes a rich stew or ragoût (usually of beef) made with beer, and is a characteristic Flemish dish.

Method
Set oven at 325°F or Mark 3. Cut the meat into 2-inch squares. Heat the dripping in a flame-proof casserole. Put in enough meat to cover the bottom and brown quickly on both sides. Remove these first pieces from the pan if there is any remaining meat to be browned. **Watchpoint** If you put too much meat into the casserole, the heat of the dripping is reduced and the meat will stew instead of fry because the juices run. If this happens, the colour of the finished dish will not be rich and brown. Do not overbrown, either, or the meat will become hard.

Remove meat, lower the heat, add the onions and cook until brown. There should be just enough fat to absorb the flour, so pour off a little of the fat if there is too much. Sprinkle in the flour, add the garlic, crushed with ½ teaspoon salt, and return

the meat to the pan. Pour the water and brown ale on the beef, add the bouquet garni, pepper, nutmeg, sugar and vinegar. Stir the pan well to clear any brown juices from the meat that might be stuck on the bottom or sides, and then cover the casserole tightly. Cook gently in the pre-set oven for 1½-2 hours. Remove the bouquet garni before serving.

Creamed potatoes

1½ lb old potatoes
1-2 oz butter
¼ pint milk
salt and pepper

Even good cooks fall down on creamed potatoes, particularly when entertaining, as they will dish them up too early and have to keep them hot. The potatoes then get an unattractive yellow skin. To prepare early and keep them hot, cook as follows.

Method
Cut the peeled potatoes in even-size pieces if very large, and put into cold salted water. Bring to the boil and cook until tender (about 20 minutes). Test with the point of a fine knife or trussing needle ; do not test with the thick prongs of a fork or the potato will break. **Watchpoint** Take care to cook potatoes in water and not let it boil away from them.

When potatoes are tender, tilt the lid of the pan and pour off all the water. Return to a gentle heat and, with the lid half-closed, continue cooking a few minutes until the potatoes are dry. Then add the butter — as much as you like — and crush the potatoes with a potato masher or a fork. Adjust seasoning. Press them down firmly to the bottom of the saucepan and pour over boiling milk ($\frac{1}{4}$ pint is enough for $1\frac{1}{2}$-2 lb potatoes). Do not stir, but put the lid on the saucepan, which should stand in a hot place until your main course is dished up. Creamed potatoes can be kept hot in this way for up to 30 minutes, and the potatoes will absorb the milk on standing. Just before dishing up, beat the potatoes very well with a wooden spoon, or small electric whisk, until fluffy.

Braised fillet of beef chasseur

2 lb fillet of beef
2 large carrots
1 large onion
1 tablespoon beef dripping, or oil
$\frac{1}{2}$ lb mushrooms
$\frac{1}{2}$ oz butter
1 shallot (finely chopped)
1 wineglass white wine
1 teaspoon tomato purée

For demi-glace sauce
2 tablespoons oil
2 tablespoons finely-diced onion, carrot and celery
$\frac{3}{4}$ oz plain flour
1 pint jellied bone stock (see page 134)
1 teaspoon tomato purée
a few mushroom peelings
bouquet garni
salt and pepper

After the second skimming, demi-glace sauce is strained before simmering for a further 5-10 minutes

Method

First prepare the demi-glace sauce (this may be done the day before if wished). Cook the vegetables in the oil until soft, then add the flour ; continue cooking very slowly to a good russet-brown. Allow mixture to cool a little, then pour on three-quarters of the stock ; return pan to the heat and stir until boiling. Add the remaining ingredients and leave to simmer very gently for about 30 minutes. Add half the reserved stock, bring to the boil and skim ; simmer for 5 minutes. Repeat this process, then strain the sauce ; return it to the rinsed pan, adjust the seasoning and continue simmering for 5-10 minutes, skimming if necessary. Set the oven at 350°F or Mark 4.

Tie the beef at regular intervals to keep it a good shape and to prevent it curling when being browned. Slice the onion and carrots into rounds. Take a heavy flameproof casserole, heat the dripping and, when it is smoking, put in the fillet and brown it on all sides ; take meat out of pan, reduce the heat and add the onion and carrot. Cover the pan and cook gently for about 10 minutes to allow the vegetables to absorb the dripping and begin to brown. Replace the meat and pour the demi-glace sauce over it ; cover with a paper and tight-fitting lid and bring to the boil. Put into a pre-set moderate oven for 20 minutes if you like your beef pink in the centre, 30 minutes if you like it well done.

Meanwhile wash and trim the mushrooms and sauté them quickly in the butter ; add the shallot, cook for 1 minute, then pour on the wine and reduce it by half. Stir in the tomato purée. Take up the beef ; slice it and arrange on the hot serving dish. Strain the sauce from the meat on to the mushroom mixture and boil up well ; taste for seasoning. Lift the mushrooms from the sauce with a draining spoon, place at each side of the dish and then moisten the meat with 2-3 tablespoons of the sauce. Serve with fondant potatoes (see page 138), the remainder of the sauce and a green vegetable.

Stufato di manzo alla romana

2 lb topside of beef
1 oz butter
1 tablespoon oil
2 onions (chopped)
2 cloves of garlic (crushed)
$\frac{1}{4}$ lb pickled pork (diced)
1 tablespoon plain flour
1 wineglass red wine
$\frac{1}{2}$-$\frac{3}{4}$ pint brown stock (see page 134)
bouquet garni
4 tomatoes (scalded and skinned)

Method

Set the oven at 350°F or Mark 4. Heat the oil and butter in a large flameproof casserole, put in the beef and brown on all sides ; take out and put in the onions, garlic and pork. Fry for about 5 minutes, draw aside, shake in the flour, brown it slightly then pour in the red wine and stock and add the bouquet garni. Season and bring to the boil. Replace the beef, cover the casserole and braise in the pre-set oven for $1\frac{1}{2}$-2 hours, basting well. Quarter the tomatoes and add them to the casserole 30 minutes before the end of the cooking time.

Take up the beef, carve and lay in a deep dish. Skim the gravy, remove the herbs, reduce gravy slightly and spoon over and round beef. Arrange polenta balls (see page 137) at each end of the dish.

Beef hot pot

4 lb skirt of beef
1 lb onions
$\frac{1}{2}$ lb mushrooms
1-2 tablespoons dripping
1-2 tablespoons plain flour
1 pint brown ale
$\frac{3}{4}$ pint good stock (see page 134)
1 teaspoon sugar
1 teaspoon wine vinegar
salt
pepper (ground from mill)
2 lb potatoes
melted butter

Method

Set oven at 350°F or Mark 4.

Cut the meat into even-sized pieces, about $1\frac{1}{2}$ inches square. Slice the onions, wash and trim the mushrooms and cut them in half. Heat the dripping in a large flameproof casserole and put in just enough meat to cover the base. When beef is nicely coloured, turn it ; when brown all over, remove it and put in more meat to brown in the same way. Reduce the heat under the pan, add the onions and cook slowly until golden-brown. Dust in enough flour to absorb the fat left in the pan and leave this to colour lightly. Add the beer and stock and stir until boiling. Add the sugar and the wine vinegar, replace the meat and season. Cover pan tightly and cook in pre-set oven for 2 hours.

Peel and slice the potatoes. Then add mushrooms to the hot pot and put potato slices on top of the meat, baste them with the juice in the pan and then brush the top with a little melted butter. Return the casserole, uncovered, to the oven and continue cooking until the top is crisp and brown (about another 45 minutes).

Beef 'en daube'

3-4 lb piece of aitchbone, or
   topside of beef
1 pigs trotter
pepper (ground from mill)
$\frac{1}{2}$ pint stock (see page 134), or water
6-8 oz salted belly pork
$\frac{3}{4}$ lb ripe tomatoes (skinned,
   seeds removed, flesh chopped)
8 green olives (stoned and sliced)

For marinade
2-3 tablespoons olive oil
1 dessertspoon wine vinegar
$\frac{1}{2}$ bottle red wine
1 onion (sliced)
1 carrot (sliced)
1 large bouquet garni (including
   bayleaf, thyme, parsley stalks and
   a strip of orange rind)
6 peppercorns
1 clove
$\frac{1}{2}$ dozen coriander seeds, or
   $\frac{1}{2}$ teaspoon ground coriander

This is a dish where the meat is first marinated and then cooked very slowly until tender. There are several variations of a daube but the essential is the long, slow, even cooking. If you have one, a heat storage cooker is ideal for this dish. Remember that a daube should be so tender that a spoon — not a knife — is used to cut the meat.

Method
Put all the ingredients for the marinade into a pan, bring slowly to the boil, then draw aside and allow to get quite cold. Place beef in a deep dish and pour over the marinade. Leave for 2-3 days (in warm weather keep meat covered in the refrigerator) turning it over several times.

Then take out the meat and strain the marinade, reserving the vegetables, herbs and spices.

Skim the oil from the surface of the marinade and put this into a thick iron or aluminium casserole large enough to hold the beef comfortably ; heat, and when the oil is hot, brown the meat and pigs trotter all over. Draw aside, add the marinade, and the reserved bouquet garni, vegetables, and the spices tied in a piece of muslin. Season with pepper only, and add the stock. Bring slowly to boil, cover and put into slow oven set at 275°F or Mark 1. Leave about 7-8 hours, when the daube should be very tender.

Meanwhile simmer the pork in water for 30-40 minutes, then take up and cut into lardons. Add these to the daube after the first 2 hours' cooking. Add the tomatoes to the daube 1 hour before the end of cooking time.

To dish up, take out the trotter, fork the meat off the bone and cut into shreds, return to the casserole with the olives, first taking out the bouquet garni. Set beef on serving dish, leave whole or slice as much as required. Reboil the gravy, skim and spoon some over the dish and serve the rest separately.

Fillet of beef italienne

3 lb fillet of beef
3 oz button mushrooms (sliced)
½ oz butter
good dripping, or butter
1 onion (quartered)
1 carrot (quartered)
bouquet garni
1 dessertspoon chopped parsley
2 oz lean cooked ham (sliced and
   shredded)

For sauce
1 shallot (finely chopped)
¼ pint white wine
½ pint demi-glace sauce (see page
   32)
1 dessertspoon tomato purée

Method

Sauté the mushrooms in the butter in a small saucepan, then take out, set aside and put the shallot and wine in the pan. Reduce to half, then add the demi-glace sauce and tomato purée. Bring to the boil and simmer for 3-4 minutes to a syrupy consistency. Cover and draw aside.

Brown the beef quickly all over in dripping or butter, with the onion and carrot, in a large pan. Then pour off any fat, add the bouquet garni and sauce. Cover tightly and simmer gently on top of stove for about 20-25 minutes (7 minutes to the lb), turning once or twice. The meat should be medium-rare.

Draw pan aside, remove bouquet garni, add the cooked mushrooms, parsley and ham. Keep pan covered until ready to serve. Serve with French beans and a dish of well-browned gnocchi romana (see opposite).

Top : adding the syrupy demi-glace sauce and tomato purée to browned fillet of beef
Above : adding cooked mushrooms, parsley and ham to medium-rare fillet of beef
Right : the finished beef italienne

Gnocchi romana

1 medium-size onion (peeled)
1 bayleaf
$\frac{1}{2}$ pint milk
$\frac{1}{2}$ pint water
5 rounded tablespoons maize meal, or coarse semolina
salt and pepper
$\frac{1}{2}$ teaspoon French mustard
1 oz butter
2 oz cheese (grated)

Method

Put onion, bayleaf, milk and water into a pan, cover and bring very slowly to the boil, to flavour the liquid. Take out onion and bayleaf.

Draw pan aside and stir in the maize meal (or semolina). Return pan to heat and stir until boiling ; season with salt and pepper, and, if too thick, add more liquid. The consistency should be that of thick porridge.

Watchpoint The amount of milk and water varies according to the type and coarseness of the maize meal used.

Continue to simmer, stirring frequently, for 7-10 minutes. Draw pan aside, adjust seasoning, then add mustard, butter and three-quarters of the grated cheese. Turn out on a tray or flat dish so that the mixture spreads to a thickness of $\frac{1}{2}$ - $\frac{3}{4}$ inch (the mixture should just pour, the consistency of very thick cream). Leave for 2-3 hours or even overnight.

Turn out the sheet of gnocchi on to a board or table and cut it into small squares, rounds or crescents. Arrange these in a well-buttered ovenproof dish in a circle, with the pieces overlapping. Sprinkle gnocchi generously with melted butter and scatter on the remaining cheese. Brown in a quick oven, pre-set at 400°F or Mark 6, for 10-15 minutes.

Sausage and tomato casserole

1½ lb pork sausages
1 large can (1¾ lb) tomatoes
2 tablespoons good dripping
2 large onions (chopped)
1 oz plain flour
2 green peppers (seeded and chopped)
salt and pepper
sugar (to taste)
1 tablespoon Worcestershire sauce
1 bayleaf
2 tablespoons browned bread-crumbs and 1 tablespoon grated Parmesan cheese (mixed)
— optional

Method

Melt the dripping in a pan, add the onion and cook slowly until golden. Blend in the flour, add the tomatoes and peppers and stir until boiling. Season, add sugar, Worcestershire sauce and the bayleaf. Simmer for 30-40 minutes.

Set oven at 375°F or Mark 5.

Meanwhile parboil the pork sausages for 10 minutes and remove their skins. Cut into thick, slanting slices.

Remove the bayleaf from the sauce. Add the sausages and tip the mixture into a pie dish. Sprinkle the top with the browned breadcrumbs and grated cheese ; bake in the pre-set oven for 30 minutes. Alternatively, if more convenient, omit the breadcrumb and cheese topping and reheat the mixture in a saucepan to boiling point before serving.

Serve with French bread.

Braised ham madère

1 gammon slipper (about 1½ lb), or small corner piece of gammon (2½-3 lb)
2 onions
2 carrots
small piece of turnip
1 stick of celery
1 oz butter
1 glass Madeira, or sherry (optional)
½ pint jellied stock (see page 134)
bouquet garni
salt and pepper

For sauce madère
2 tablespoons oil, or dripping
1 rounded tablespoon plain flour
1¼ pint clear brown jellied stock (flavoured with vegetables) — see page 134
½ teaspoon tomato purée
1 glass Madeira, or golden sherry

Tammy strainer

Method

Soak gammon in cold water for 12 hours, then drain and parboil it in fresh water : 30 minutes for a slipper, 1 hour for a corner piece.

Set oven at 325°F or Mark 3.

Slice vegetables and cook gently in butter, drain cooked gammon and place on top.

Pour over 1 glass of Madeira or sherry, if used, and set alight to drive off alcohol. Add stock, bouquet garni and seasoning. Cover with greaseproof paper and lid, braise gently in pre-set oven for 1 hour.

To prepare sauce : melt fat, stir in flour and cook until straw coloured, add stock and tomato purée. Simmer for at least 45 minutes, skimming frequently. When well reduced and clear, strain sauce through a tammy strainer, boil the Madeira or sherry to reduce by half and add to the sauce.

Skin and slice ham, arrange on serving dish on a bed of spinach à la crème (see right), spoon over the sauce and serve with creamed potatoes (see page 30), or with new potatoes tossed in butter and chopped parsley.

The 'fonds' or braising juice, if not too fat or salty, may be reduced and added to the sauce.

Spinach à la crème

1½ lb spinach
½ oz butter
5 tablespoons double cream, or
    béchamel sauce (see page 136)
salt and pepper
little grated nutmeg

Method

Wash spinach until completely clean. Cook in plenty of boiling salted water for about 8-10 minutes. Drain well and press between two plates to remove any excess water. Rub through a wire strainer or Mouli sieve.

Melt butter in a pan until slightly coloured, add spinach and cook for a few minutes until dry. Then add cream or béchamel sauce and heat thoroughly. Season carefully and add a little grated nutmeg.

Ham madère is served, sliced, on a bed of spinach à la crème with the rich sauce madère poured round it

Stuffed pork fillet

3-4 pork fillets (total weight 1¾-2 lb)
1 oz butter
1 glass (2½ fl oz) sherry, or stock
(see page 134)
1 tablespoon plain flour
½ pint stock
salt and pepper

For stuffing
2 oz butter
1 medium-size onion (finely
chopped)
8 oz minced veal
1 dessertspoon chopped parsley
1 teaspoon mixed herbs
1 teaspoon sage
grated rind and juice of ½ lemon
1 cup fresh white breadcrumbs
salt and pepper
1 egg (beaten)

Method

Split the fillets two-thirds of the way through and beat with a heavy knife to flatten — many butchers sell the pork fillet cut and dressed in this way.

Set oven at 350°F or Mark 4.

To prepare stuffing : cook the onion in the butter until soft but not coloured, add to the other ingredients in a bowl and add enough beaten egg to bind.

Layer this stuffing between the filets, shaping them to form a loaf ; tie up with fine string or secure with poultry pins. Heat the butter in a flameproof casserole, or stewpan, and brown the pork carefully on both sides. Pour over the sherry (or stock), cover with greaseproof paper and lid, and cook in the pre-set oven for 2 hours.

Take up the meat and keep warm while preparing the gravy. Blend the flour into the butter and juices in the pan and cook slowly until russet-brown, tip in the stock and stir until boiling. Season with salt and pepper, simmer for 2-3 minutes and

Below : layering stuffing between beaten pork fillets. Right : browning shaped fillets before putting in oven with sherry or stock

strain. Remove the string or skewers from the pork and serve whole or sliced. Spoon a little gravy round the meat and pour the rest into a sauce boat.

Potatoes, parsnips and brussels sprouts are good with this dish.

Stuffed pork fillet

with celery and onion fondue

2 fillets of pork (about 12 oz each)
1 oz butter
3 large onions (preferably Spanish)
— sliced
1 head of celery (sliced)
about ½ pint good stock (page 134)
1 small carton (2½ fl oz) single cream
little slaked arrowroot (optional)

For stuffing
6 oz pork (minced)
1 medium-size onion (finely
chopped)
1 oz butter
2 oz fresh white breadcrumbs
1 rounded dessertspoon freshly
chopped sage, or 1 teaspoon dry
chopped sage
1 rounded dessertspoon chopped
parsley
salt and pepper
1 egg yolk, or 1 small egg (beaten)

Method

First prepare the stuffing. Soften the onion in the butter without colouring, and turn into a bowl with the minced pork, crumbs, sage, parsley and seasoning. Mix well and bind with the egg.

Remove any skin from the pork fillets and split down the centre to open them out. Then lay each fillet between 2 pieces of waxed or greaseproof paper, and beat them slightly to flatten.

Spread the stuffing on one of the fillets and cover with the other, arranging them head to tail. Roll slightly to neaten shape, and sew up or fasten with poultry pins, or tie with string.

Set oven at 350°F or Mark 4.

Heat a flameproof casserole or braising pan, drop in about 1 oz butter and then put in the pork to brown on both sides. Take out, put in onions and celery and cook for 5-6 minutes, stirring fairly frequently.

Replace the pork on the top, pour round the stock, cover tightly and braise in the pre-set oven for about 40-45 minutes.

Take up the pork, lift out the onion and celery with a draining spoon and arrange down a serving dish. Remove the pins or string from the pork, slice and arrange on top of the vegetables.

Adjust the seasoning of the gravy, boil up and add the cream. Continue to boil for 1-2 minutes until syrupy, and then spoon over the dish. Serve with creamed potatoes (see page 30). **Note :** it is not usual here to thicken the gravy, but if wished it could be slightly thickened with a little slaked arrowroot.

1 Spreading stuffing on one pork fillet before covering with other fillet
2 Sewing up stuffed pork fillet before braising with vegetables
3 The finished stuffed pork fillet with the celery and onion fondue

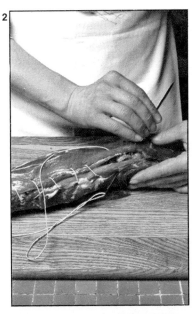

Pork chops in ginger ale

4-5 large pork chops
2 large onions (sliced)
2 oz butter, or 1 oz butter and 1 oz dripping
little brown sugar
1 tablespoon tomato purée
1 tablespoon plain flour
$\frac{1}{2}$ pint ginger ale
salt and pepper

Method

Set oven at 350°F or Mark 4. Sauté the onions in a pan with half the butter until golden-brown ; remove them and place in an ovenproof casserole.

Brown the pork chops well on both sides in remaining butter (or dripping) in a pan, then place them on top of the onions. Scatter over a little brown sugar.

Mix the tomato purée and flour together in a basin and add the ginger ale ; pour this over the chops and season. Put in pre-set oven for about 1 hour or until chops are tender.

Serve with white cabbage ; just before draining, add 2 oz cooked shredded ham and finely chopped green pepper ; drain and serve very hot.

Polpette alla milanese

1 pork fillet, or tenderloin (weighing about 12 oz)
4 oz minced pork
4 oz sausage meat
1 clove of garlic (crushed with a little salt)
1 teaspoon chopped parsley
1 tablespoon grated Parmesan cheese
black pepper
little grated nutmeg
1 egg (beaten)
about $\frac{1}{4}$ lb green streaky bacon (cut at No. 4)
1 tablespoon seasoned flour
2 oz clarified butter (see page 141)
1 wineglass white wine

Method

Cut the pork fillet into thin slices and bat out with a rolling pin or a bottle. Mix the minced pork, sausage meat, garlic, parsley, cheese and seasoning together, and add a little beaten egg to bind. Spread out the bacon rashers with a knife blade. Put a layer of the stuffing mixture on to each slice of pork, roll up, wrap in a slice of the bacon and fasten with a cock-tail stick. Dust with a little seasoned flour.

Set oven at 350°F or Mark 4. Heat the butter, in a flameproof casserole, put in the pork rolls and cook gently until golden-brown all over. Pour over the white wine and allow to reduce to half quantity, then cover the pan tightly and put in the pre-set moderate oven for 30-40 minutes. Serve this with a risotto milanese (see opposite) and a green vegetable.

Risotto milanese

8 oz thick grain rice (preferably Italian)
1 marrow bone (optional)
2 oz butter
1 small onion (finely chopped)
1 clove of garlic (chopped, or crushed, with $\frac{1}{2}$ teaspoon salt)
1 pinch of saffron (soaked in 2 tablespoons hot water) — optional
about 1$\frac{1}{4}$ pints chicken, or veal, stock (see page 134)
salt and pepper
2-3 tablespoons grated Parmesan cheese

Sliced mushrooms (2-3 oz) are sometimes added to this risotto with the onion. For special occasions, use a glass of white wine in place of the same amount of stock.

The quantity of rice given here is enough for a main course for four people. For a first course, 5-6 oz of rice is sufficient, with the remaining ingredients in proportion.

Method

Scoop out marrow from the bone and cut in small pieces. Melt a good half of the butter in a shallow pan or flameproof casserole, add marrow, onion and garlic. Fry gently for 4-5 minutes, add rice and continue to fry, stirring continually until all the grains look white — 4-5 minutes.

Then add saffron in its liquid and about a third of the stock. Season and simmer, stirring occasionally until the rice thickens, then add another third of the stock. Continue in this way until the grains are barely tender and the risotto creamy.

Draw pan aside, dot the surface with the remaining butter and sprinkle with 1-2 tablespoons of Parmesan cheese. Cover rice and leave for 5 minutes, or until ready to serve. Stir once or twice with a fork, then turn into a hot dish. Avoid touching with a spoon as this makes it mushy.

Note : bone marrow is characteristic of a risotto milanese but both it and the saffron may be omitted. If more convenient, the marrow bone may be boiled before scooping out the marrow, which is then added to the risotto towards the end of cooking. In either case the bone can be used for stock.

Salt pork
with sauerkraut and frankfurters

1½ lb salt belly of pork
2 oz butter
1½ lb sauerkraut (fresh or canned)
1 medium-size onion (stuck with a clove)
1 carrot (peeled)
2-3 tablespoons dry white wine, or stock (see page 134), or water
salt and pepper
little kneaded butter

For garnish
2 pairs of frankfurter sausages (poached)
boiled potatoes

Method

Put pork in a large pan, cover with cold water, bring slowly to the boil, simmer gently for about 1 hour, and leave to cool in the liquid. Set the oven at 350°F or Mark 4.

Well grease an ovenproof casserole with half of the butter, arrange the sauerkraut in this with the onion and carrot. Put the pork in the centre, moisten with the liquid, season, and cover with buttered paper.

Cover the casserole with a tightly fitting lid and cook in pre-set oven for about 1½ hours. At end of cooking time liquid should have evaporated.

Take out the pork, bind the sauerkraut with a little kneaded butter, reheat, stirring constantly, and add remaining butter.

Slice the pork and serve on the sauerkraut, garnished with the cooked frankfurters and boiled potatoes. The onion and carrot may be sliced and mixed with the sauerkraut if wished.

Salt pork is served with sauerkraut, frankfurters and boiled potatoes

Ossi buchi

2 lb shin of veal (cut in slices
  2 inches thick)
1 oz butter
1 onion (sliced)
1 carrot (sliced)
1 wineglass white wine
½ lb tomatoes
1 dessertspoon tomato purée
1 clove of garlic (crushed with
  ½ teaspoon salt)
½-¾ pint of jellied bone stock (see
  page 134)
bouquet garni
1 tablespoon chopped parsley

Method

Brown the veal in the butter and lift carefully out of the pan. Add the onion and carrot, cover the pan and cook over a steady heat, without stirring, for 2-3 minutes. Put the veal back into the pan, making sure that the bones remain upright so the marrow does not fall out as the meat cooks. Pour over the white wine and allow to reduce to half quantity.

Meanwhile scald and skin the tomatoes, cut away the hard core, squeeze to remove a certain amount of the seeds and chop the flesh finely. Add this to the pan with the tomato purée and cook for 10-15 minutes. Then add the garlic, stock and bouquet garni. Cover and cook for 1½ hours.

Take up the veal and arrange in a serving dish. Tip the contents of the pan into a conical strainer and press well. **Watchpoint** All the tomato pulp should go through the strainer but the carrots and onion should remain behind. Reduce this sauce rapidly until syrupy, adjust the seasoning, spoon over the veal, dust with the chopped parsley and serve with a risotto milanese (see page 45).

Braised veal Orloff

2½ lb fillet of veal
1 oz butter
1 large onion (diced)
2 carrots (diced)
1 stick of celery (diced)
1 wineglass white wine
¼ pint stock (see page 134)
salt and pepper
bouquet garni
1 rounded teaspoon arrowroot
   (mixed with 1 tablespoon cold
   water)

For soubise
2 large onions (chopped)
½ oz butter
3 oz Carolina rice
¼ pint stock
salt and pepper
1 egg yolk
1 tablespoon single cream

For mornay sauce
1 oz butter
1 rounded tablespoon plain flour
½ pint milk
2-3 tablespoons grated cheese
1 tablespoon single cream

To garnish
8 oz mushrooms
¼ oz butter
salt and pepper
squeeze of lemon juice

Braised veal Orloff is a classic veal dish but it adapts well for loin of lamb. Order a 3 lb loin of lamb and ask the butcher to chine the meat ; it is then quite easy to cut away not only the backbone but every small chop bone.

Method

Set oven at 350°F or Mark 4.

Tie the veal neatly with string to keep it a good shape while cooking. Melt the butter in a flameproof casserole, add the diced vegetables and set the meat on top. Cover the dish and cook for 30 minutes in the pre-set oven.

Pour over the white wine, cover the casserole again, return to the oven and continue cooking to reduce the wine (allow 30 minutes for this). Pour over the stock, which should come half-way up the meat, season, tuck in the bouquet garni by the meat and cover with greaseproof paper and the lid.

Lower the oven to 325°F or Mark 3 and cook the veal for 2 hours.

Meanwhile prepare the soubise, mornay sauce and garnish.

To prepare the soubise : cook the chopped onion gently in the butter until soft but not coloured, add the rice and stock and season. Bring to the boil, cover and cook in the oven for about 30 minutes, until very soft.

Watchpoint You must overcook rice so that each grain will split. Rub it through a wire strainer or mix to a purée in an electric blender. Then stir in the egg yolk and cream.

To prepare the mornay sauce : melt butter, remove from heat, add the flour and blend in milk, then return to heat and stir until boiling. Cook for 2 minutes, cool, then gradually beat in the cheese and cream. Cover with a buttered greaseproof paper to prevent a skin forming.

Trim and wash the mushrooms and cook for 1-2 minutes in $\frac{1}{4}$ oz butter, salt and pepper and a squeeze of lemon.

Take veal out of oven and keep warm. Strain the stock from the veal in the pan and thicken lightly with the arrowroot mixture. Taste for seasoning before setting aside for gravy.

Carve the meat, spread each slice with the soubise purée and reshape the joint on the serving dish. Spoon over the mornay sauce and brown in the oven at 400°F or Mark 6 for 12-15 minutes. Pour a little of the gravy round the meat and garnish with the mushrooms. Hand round gravy separately. Serve with boiled rice (see page 139) and brussels sprouts.

Note : if making this dish the day before for a party, carve, stuff and reshape joint on party day ; after coating with mornay sauce allow 30-40 minutes in the oven at 350°F or Mark 4.

Breast of veal with tomatoes

2½-3 lb breast of veal (boned)
about 2 oz butter, or bacon fat
1 oz sliced onions
1 oz sliced carrots
1 oz sliced celery
bouquet garni
1 pint strong veal stock (made
  from bones — see page 134)
¼ pint strong fresh tomato pulp,
  or tomato purée diluted with stock
salt and pepper
kneaded butter
2½-3½ fl oz double cream

For marinade
black pepper (ground from mill)
pinch of ground mace
grated rind of ½ lemon
squeeze of lemon
2 wineglasses white wine

For farce
1 small onion (chopped)
1 oz butter
½ lb minced pork
3 oz fresh white breadcrumbs
1 heaped tablespoon chopped
  mixed herbs
1 small egg (beaten)

For garnish
4-6 tomatoes (halved)
4-6 bacon rashers

Ask your butcher to bone out
the veal and give you the bones
to make the stock.

Method
Lay the veal in a shallow dish,
grind over a little black pepper
and sprinkle with a good pinch
of mace. Grate over the lemon
rind, add lemon juice and pour
over the wine. Cover and leave
overnight to marinate.

Set oven at 350°F or Mark 4.

To prepare farce: soften
onion in a pan with the butter,
add to the pork with the breadcrumbs and herbs, then bind
with the beaten egg. Take up
the veal, wipe it dry and spread
the farce over it, roll and tie up.
Reserve the marinade.

Melt the butter (or bacon fat)
in a large flameproof casserole,
put in the veal and brown slowly,
then remove meat and sauté
the vegetables without colouring.
Replace the veal and add the
marinade. Allow this to reduce
by half, then put in the bouquet
garni and pour round two-thirds
of the stock. Bring to the boil,
cover and braise in pre-set oven
for 1½-2 hours; baste occasionally.

After 1 hour, remove the lid
and continue to cook, basting
from time to time and adding
the rest of the stock if necessary.
When veal is tender and well
glazed, take it out, remove the
bouquet garni and rub the
contents of the pan through a
fine sieve, or work in a blender.
Add the tomato pulp to this,
turn mixture into a saucepan
and bring to the boil. Adjust
seasoning, thicken lightly with
kneaded butter and boil gently
for 5 minutes. Add the cream
and continue to boil until
thoroughly blended.

Meanwhile bake the tomatoes
and bake or grill the rashers.
Remove trussing strings from
the veal, dish up and spoon
over a little of the sauce. Serve
the rest separately in a sauce
boat. Garnish the dish with the
tomatoes and bacon. Accompany
with dauphinois potatoes (see
page 138).

Spreading the farce on the breast of veal before rolling it up and tying with string preparatory to browning

Dishing up breast of veal ; the meat is sliced and arranged on the dish with the tomatoes and bacon

Breast of veal with tomatoes and bacon has a little of the sauce spooned over the slices of meat for serving. Remaining sauce is served separately.

Veal sauté chasseur

1½ lb fillet, or oyster, of veal
4 oz mushrooms
2 tablespoons oil
1 oz butter
4 shallots
1 tablespoon plain flour
2 wineglasses white wine
½-¾ pint stock (see page 134)
1 dessertspoon tomato purée
bouquet garni

To garnish
1 teaspoon chopped chervil
triangular croûtes of fried bread

Method
Cut the meat into 1-1½ inch cubes. Wash and trim the mushrooms and cut them into slices. Heat the oil in a heavy flameproof casserole, add the butter and, when melted, put in the meat a few pieces at a time and cook until golden-brown on all sides. Remove the meat from the pan.

Watchpoint For this dish it is important that the pieces of veal should be allowed to colour without being disturbed, and certainly do not allow one piece of meat to fall on top of another. You will find it necessary to cook the meat in two or more batches.

When all the meat is coloured, remove it from the pan and keep it warm. Reduce the heat under the casserole a little, add the mushrooms and sauté them for 2-3 minutes until all the water has been driven off. Tip off any fat left in the pan, add the shallot and dust with the flour ; mix well and then cook for about 5 minutes, stirring from time to time, until the flour is a good russet-brown. Add the wine and stock, a little at a time, and cook until smooth. Add the tomato purée and bouquet garni ; return the meat to the pan and bring to the boil. Cover the pan with a well-fitting lid and cook gently in a moderate oven, pre-set at 350°F or Mark 4, for about 1½ hours. For serving, dish up meat, reduce the sauce, adjust the seasoning, and spoon over the meat. Dust with the chopped chervil and surround with the croûtes.

Braised stuffed veal

3 lb breast, or loin, of veal
(with kidney)
1 oz butter
2 oz green streaky bacon (cut
into cubes)
1 large onion (sliced)
2 carrots (sliced)
$\frac{1}{2}$-$\frac{3}{4}$ pint stock (see page 134)

For stuffing
1 shallot, or small onion (chopped)
1 oz butter
1 lb pork sausage meat
1 teaspoon mixed chopped herbs
salt and pepper

Method
Set oven at 325°F or Mark 3. Bone the veal. Skin and trim the kidney but leave it whole.

To prepare the stuffing : cook the shallot (or onion) in the butter until soft but not coloured, then add it to the sausage meat with the herbs and seasoning. Spread this mixture over the meat and put the kidney in the centre. Roll the meat up and tie securely with string.

Brown the veal slowly in the butter until well coloured on all sides. Remove it from the pan and put in the bacon ; cook slowly until beginning to colour, then add the sliced onion and carrot. Cover the pan and leave over moderate heat for 5 minutes. Do not stir during this time.

Then replace the veal on the bed of vegetables, pour over the stock, cover the meat with a double sheet of greaseproof paper, put the lid on and cook in pre-set moderate oven for about 2 hours. (Allow 30 minutes per lb total weight, ie. veal including stuffing.)

Take up the meat, remove the string, strain the stock in the pan through a conical strainer, pressing the vegetables well against the sides. Either reduce the stock to thicken it a little or bind with 1 teaspoon arrowroot mixed to a paste with a little water. Reboil, test for seasoning and spoon gravy over the meat.

Blanquette of veal

2¼ lb breast of veal
2 medium-size carrots (quartered)
2 medium-size onions (quartered)
1 bouquet garni
pinch of salt
1½ pints stock (see page 134).
 or water

For sauce
1½ oz butter
3 tablespoons plain flour
1-2 egg yolks
¼ pint creamy milk
squeeze of lemon juice

Traditionally, breast of veal is used for this dish to get a rich, jellied stock from bones. But a greater proportion of shoulder meat can be added, ie. twice as much as breast. Breast of lamb can replace the veal.

Method

Cut meat into chunks (ask your butcher to do this if you are using breast of lamb and also trim off excess fat — otherwise cook in the same way). Soak overnight in cold water, blanch, drain and refresh.

Put the meat into a large pan with the quartered carrots and onions. Add bouquet garni, salt and barely cover with the stock or water. Cover and simmer for 1-1¼ hours until very tender and a bone can be pulled from a piece of meat.

Draw pan aside and pour off all liquid, cover pan and keep hot. The stock should measure 1 pint. If it is more, turn into a pan and boil to reduce to 1 pint.

To prepare the sauce : melt the butter in a separate pan, stir in the flour, cook for 1-2 seconds without letting the butter brown, draw aside and allow to cool slightly. Pour on the stock, blend, then stir until boiling. Boil briskly for 3-4 minutes until sauce is creamy in consistency and then draw aside.

Mix yolks with milk in a bowl, add a little of the hot sauce, then pour mixture slowly back into the bulk of the sauce. Taste for seasoning and add the lemon juice. Pour sauce over veal, shake pan gently to mix all together. Cover and keep hot for 15 minutes before serving so that the flavour of the sauce can penetrate the meat. Turn meat and vegetables into a clean hot dish and serve with creamed potatoes (see page 30) or boiled rice (see page 139).

For a party dish, single cream instead of milk can be used for the sauce, but if you decide to to do this, take out the onions and carrots before serving and replace them with a mixture of previously cooked peas, baby carrots and button onions.

Offal dishes

Foods that are classed as offal are often much maligned, and casseroles and braises probably bring out the best in them. The flavour in most offal is rich and distinctive, but the meat is often tough and needs slow cooking to make it tender. Try grilling oxtail or heart and your family will really wish the butcher had never offered it for sale ! And even kidney and liver, which are so popular in grills, also lend themselves remarkably well to oven dishes.

All offal, especially liver, heart and kidneys, should be very fresh when cooked. It is advisable to buy it the day you intend to cook it ; if you do need to store it in the refrigerator for a short time, make sure it is completely covered, as some offal has a rather strong smell and might taint other foods stored there.

Oxtail makes an excellent, inexpensive dish, especially for winter. It is usually braised or made into a nourishing soup. When buying, choose one that has an equal amount of meat to bone. It is sold jointed and the fat must be white, the meat bright red. An average-size tail is enough for four people.

Liver needs no special preparation, so long as it is fresh and clean-looking and has little or no smell.

Hearts make another cheap and nourishing dish. Our recipe on page 59 is for lambs hearts, and you will need one per person. Calves, or pigs, hearts may be prepared in the same way, but call for long and careful cooking to make them tender ; one of these is sufficient for two people.

Tongues vary in size, depending whether they are from lamb, calf, or ox. The most common dish is salted ox tongue, served cold, but tongues can equally well be braised and eaten hot — lambs tongues are always served this way.

All tongues are improved by soaking in cold water for 2-3 hours. Then rinse them well by putting in a roomy pan of cold water, bringing to the boil and draining. Return them to the pan, cover with cold water and add a few root vegetables and a bouquet garni for flavouring. Simmer until the tongues are three-parts cooked (lambs tongues take about 1 hour) ; remove from the pan and plunge into a bowl of cold water. Nick the skin on the underside of the tongues and peel off carefully. Trim away some of the fat of necessary and they are then ready for braising.

Lambs tongues weigh 4-6 oz each ; allow at least 1 per person — say 6 tongues of average size for 4 people. Calves tongues average 12 oz - 1 lb in weight and are sweet, tender and delicate in flavour.

Tripe makes an easily digested. nourishing dish but again must be carefully prepared and cooked. The lining of a bullock's stomach, tripe is sold ready cleaned and blanched. After this it needs long, slow cooking to make it tender.

Sweetbreads must be eaten really fresh. Before cooking, soak them for several hours in salted water ; 1-2 slices of lemon or a few drops of vinegar may be added to the water. Rinse breads, put into a pan and cover with cold water, add a little salt and a slice of lemon. Bring slowly to the boil, removing any scum as it rises to the surface. Drain, rinse quickly, then remove any ducts or 'pipes' and any skin, which will pull off easily. Lay breads on a flat dish or tray, with another tray on top. Set a light weight (approximately 2 lb) on this and leave breads until quite cold. They are then ready for braising.

Lambs breads are small and are sold by the pound — allow about 4-6 oz per person and 4-6 oz over. Calves breads are much larger, weighing about 6 oz each. They are usually sold by the pair ; allow 2-3 pairs for 4 people. There is little wastage.

Braised oxtail

1 oxtail (jointed)
dripping
2 onions (peeled)
2 carrots (peeled and quartered)
3 sticks of celery (cut in 2-inch
  lengths)
1 tablespoon plain flour
about 1 pint stock (see page 134)
  or water
bouquet garni
salt and pepper

Method

Set the oven at 350°F or Mark 4. Brown the pieces of tail all over in hot dripping in a flameproof casserole. Take out ; put in the onions, carrots and celery. Leave to brown lightly, then dust in the flour. Remove from heat, add the liquid, bring to the boil, add bouquet garni and seasoning.

Put in the tail, cover casserole tightly and cook in the pre-set oven for about $1\frac{1}{2}$-2 hours or until tender (when the meat will come easily off the bone). Remove the bouquet garni and serve meat very hot.

Watchpoint Sometimes oxtail is inclined to be fatty so it is a good plan to cook it the day before, leave to go cold, then skim off the solidified fat. Reheat for serving.

Braised liver with mushrooms

1½ lb calves, or lambs, liver (in the piece)
2 wineglasses dry white wine
salt and pepper
bouquet garni
1 medium-size onion (sliced)
4 large tomatoes
5 rashers unsmoked bacon collar (No. 4 cut)
3 oz butter
1 tablespoon plain flour
½ lb small, flat mushrooms
2-3 tablespoons olive oil
3 shallots (very finely chopped)

Trussing needle and string, or small skewers

Method

Mix together the wine, seasoning, bouquet garni and onion. Pour this marinade over the liver and leave for about 1½ hours ; turn and baste two or three times.

Scald and skin the tomatoes, remove the seeds and chop flesh finely.

Set the oven at 350°F or Mark 4. Take the liver from the marinade, drain and wipe dry with absorbent paper. Strain and reserve the marinade.

Remove the rind and rust from the bacon, wrap round the liver and secure with trussing needle and string, or skewers.

Heat half the butter in a flameproof casserole or cocotte (an enamelled or cast iron dish) and brown liver on all sides. Remove, keep warm, and pour away any fat before wiping casserole well. Melt the remaining butter, stir in the flour and cook gently until it is straw-coloured and marbled in appearance, then add tomatoes and strained marinade. Bring to the boil, put in the liver and cook in the pre-set oven for about 30 minutes.

Wash and trim the mushrooms. Heat the oil in a frying pan, add the mushrooms and cook quickly for 1 minute, lower heat, add the shallots and cook for a further 1-2 minutes. Put mushroom mixture in casserole, cook for a further 20-30 minutes until liver is tender.

For serving, remove the string or skewers and slice the liver. Replace it in casserole or arrange on a hot serving dish. Pour on sauce and mushrooms. Serve with creamed potatoes (see page 30).

Casserole of liver

1-1½ lb lambs liver
6 rashers streaky bacon
½-1 oz butter, or dripping
4 oz mushrooms
3 medium-size onions (sliced)
1 tablespoon plain flour
¾ pint stock (see page 134)
salt and pepper
12 black olives (stoned)
squeeze of lemon juice

Method

Set the oven at 350°F or Mark 4.
  Slice the liver and cut bacon into small pieces. Fry bacon first in butter or dripping in a pan. Take out and put in liver ; sauté for 2 minutes on each side until brown. Take out and arrange in a casserole.
  Wipe out pan, sauté mushrooms for 3 minutes in a little extra dripping ; take out, set aside. Fry onions until golden-brown, add with bacon to liver.
  Dust flour into pan, make a roux. Pour on stock and bring to boil. Season, strain into casserole, cover and cook gently for 40-50 minutes in the pre-set oven. Then add mushrooms and olives, finish with lemon juice. Return to oven for 10 minutes before serving.

Braised lambs hearts

4-5 lambs hearts
1 oz butter, or dripping
2 large onions (thinly sliced)
salt and pepper
¾ pint stock (see page 134)
kneaded butter, or arrowroot, or cornflour (mixed with a little cold water) — to thicken

For herb stuffing
5 tablespoons fresh white breadcrumbs
2 tablespoons chopped mixed herbs, or parsley and 1 teaspoon dried herbs
salt and pepper
1 small egg (beaten)

Trussing needle and fine string, or thread

Method

Trim hearts with scissors, cutting away any fat and blood vessels ; snip the wall dividing the interior of the heart. Soak them for about 1 hour in salted water. Dry thoroughly.
  Set the oven at 350°F or Mark 4. Mix the ingredients for the stuffing, adding enough egg to moisten. Stuff the hearts and sew up the openings with fine string or thread.
  Brown the hearts in butter or dripping in a flameproof casserole, take out of the pan, put in the onions, cook them until brown, then set the hearts on top. Season, add the stock, cover with foil and then put on the lid. Braise in the pre-set oven for 1½ hours, or until very tender.
  Dish up and thicken the liquid slightly with kneaded butter, or arrowroot, or cornflour. Pour over the hearts and serve very hot.

Braised lambs tongues florentine

6 lambs tongues
3 rashers of streaky bacon (unsmoked)
2 onions
2 carrots
1 stick of celery
bouquet garni
6 white peppercorns
$\frac{1}{2}$ pint jellied stock (see page 134)

For sauce
1 oz butter
1 shallot, or small onion (finely grated)
1 rounded tablespoon plain flour
$\frac{1}{4}$ pint jellied stock
1 dessertspoon tomato purée
1 glass brown sherry

For serving
spinach creams (see page 140)
1 lb potatoes (cooked and beaten to a purée with $\frac{1}{2}$ oz butter, 4 tablespoons hot milk, salt and pepper)

Method

Blanch and refresh the tongues, put in pan with enough water to cover, then simmer gently for $1\frac{1}{4}$-$1\frac{1}{2}$ hours. Drain the tongues, plunge them into a bowl of cold water and skin them. Trim and cut away the root.

Set oven at 350°F or Mark 4.

Remove the rind from the bacon, stretch each rasher under the blade of a heavy knife and place them at bottom of a flameproof casserole. Slice the onions, carrots and celery, put in the casserole and cover. Cook over gentle heat for 10-12 minutes or until the bacon starts to brown. Place the tongues on top of the vegetables, add bouquet garni, peppercorns and the $\frac{1}{2}$ pint of stock. Cover the tongues with a double thickness of greaseproof paper and lid and braise for 45 minutes in oven.

Watchpoint This braising is to give the tongues extra flavour, but they must be quite tender before the process is started, so do not cut the initial stewing time.

To prepare the sauce : melt the butter, add shallot or onion and cook slowly for 2 minutes ; stir in the flour and continue cooking until onion and flour are deep brown. Draw pan off the heat, blend in $\frac{1}{2}$ pint of the stock, the tomato purée and sherry ; return to the heat and stir until boiling. Then, with the lid half off the pan, simmer gently for 15-20 minutes. Pour in half the remaining stock, skim sauce and reboil ; simmer for 5 minutes. Pour rest of stock into sauce, skim again and simmer for a further 5 minutes. Strain, cover and set aside.

Take up tongues, strain off the braising liquid, return it to the pan and boil hard until it is reduced by half. Add the sauce to this liquid, taste for seasoning and boil up together. Return tongues to casserole and keep warm while beating the potato purée and taking up the spinach creams.

To serve : place the potato purée in the serving dish, take up the tongues, slice in half and arrange on top. Turn out the spinach creams and place round the dish. Boil up the sauce and spoon over just enough to coat the tongues and the base of the dish ; serve the rest separately in a sauce boat.

Lambs tongues on potato purée, coated with sauce and surrounded by moulded spinach creams

Trimming away the roof of a tongue ; the tongue in the foreground is already trimmed

Placing the trimmed lambs tongues on top of the sliced onions, carrots and celery for braising

Braised tongues bigarade

2 calves tongues, or 3 lb fresh ox tongue

For mirepoix (for braising)
2 onions
2 carrots
1 small turnip
1 stick of celery
1 tablespoon dripping, or butter
about ½ pint jellied stock (see page 134)
bouquet garni

For ½ pint demi-glace sauce
2 tablespoons oil
2 tablespoons finely chopped onion, carrot and celery (mixed)
1 tablespoon plain flour
¾ pint brown bone stock
few mushroom peelings
½ teaspoon tomato purée
bouquet garni
salt and pepper

For bigarade sauce
2 shallots (finely chopped)
nut of butter
1 wineglass red wine
small bayleaf
rind and juice of 1 orange (preferably Seville)
½ pint demi-glace sauce (as above)
1 teaspoon redcurrant jelly

This is a good party recipe as the whole dish can be prepared ahead of time and left ready for reheating.

Method

Soak the tongue or tongues in salted water for 24 hours. Then blanch and simmer for $1\frac{1}{2}$-2 hours.

Set the oven at 300°F or Mark 3. Trim and skin the tongues. Dice the vegetables for the mirepoix and cook slowly in the dripping, or butter, in a heavy flameproof casserole until they are coloured, then place the prepared tongue on the top and pour over the jellied stock. Add the bouquet garni, cover the pan, bring to the boil and then cook in pre-set moderate oven for about $1\frac{1}{2}$-2 hours, or until very tender.

Meanwhile prepare the demi-glace sauce (see method, page 32).

To make bigarade sauce: chop the shallots finely and soften them in butter in a small pan. Add the wine and bayleaf. Reduce gently by about one-third. Add to the demi-glace sauce, together with the juice and half the pared orange rind. Simmer for 5-7 minutes.

Shred remaining orange rind

Adding stock to tongues for braised tongues bigarade

thinly, blanch for 5 minutes, and drain. Strain sauce and return to pan with shredded rind and redcurrant jelly. Bring slowly to boil, stirring frequently to dissolve the jelly.

Note : to be correct, this sauce should have a small bitter or Seville orange rather than a sweet one. If, however, the latter has to be used, sharpen the sauce with a few drops of lemon juice.

Take up the tongue, and cut in $\frac{1}{4}$-inch diagonal slices. Strain other contents from pan, replace tongue in the braising pan and pour over the strained stock. To finish the tongue, return pan to oven, without the lid, and continue cooking for about 30 minutes, basting tongue with stock from time to time. This gives it a glazed appearance.

Pour a little bigarade sauce over tongue. Serve with purée of celeriac and potato. Serve the remaining sauce separately.

Purée of celeriac and potato

1 medium-size head of celeriac
$\frac{3}{4}$-1 lb potatoes
$\frac{1}{2}$ oz butter
salt and pepper
little hot milk

Method
Peel celeriac and cut into eight pieces. Peel potatoes and, if large, cut them in half. Boil celeriac and potatoes together in salted water until both are tender ; then drain and dry them thoroughly before mashing with butter and seasoning.

Beat well, adding a little hot milk, until it is light and fluffy.

Tripe Italian style

$1\frac{1}{2}$ lb tripe
$\frac{1}{2}$ pint milk and 1 pint water (salted)
6 tablespoons olive oil
1 large onion (sliced)
2 oz flat mushrooms (chopped)
1 bayleaf
1 lb tomatoes (skinned and finely chopped), or 2 tablespoons tomato purée
1 clove of garlic (crushed with $\frac{1}{2}$ teaspoon salt)
$\frac{1}{4}$ pint white wine, or dry cider
1 tablespoon chopped parsley
pinch of dried rosemary, or oregano
grate of nutmeg
salt and pepper
about $\frac{1}{4}$- $\frac{1}{2}$ pint stock (see page 134), or water

Method
Cook the tripe in salted milk and water for 1 hour, then drain and cut into fine strips, $3\frac{1}{2}$-4 inches long.

Put the oil in a deep pan, add the onion and when beginning to colour add the mushrooms ; after 1 minute add the tripe.

Put in the bayleaf, tomatoes or tomato purée, garlic and wine or cider, herbs and spices. Season, cover pan and simmer very gently for about 1 hour until tripe is very tender.

If stew shows signs of drying, add a little stock or water from time to time. The consistency should be thick and rich.

Serve with boiled potatoes.

Lambs sweetbreads bonne maman

1½ lb (2 pairs) lambs sweetbreads
1 oz butter
¾ oz plain flour
¾ pint veal, or chicken, stock (see page 134)
1 teaspoon tomato purée
salt and pepper
4 oz cooked ham (shredded)
1 teaspoon chopped parsley
2-3 tablespoons double cream
creamed potatoes (for piping border) — see page 30
grated Parmesan cheese (optional)

For julienne
1 oz butter
2 medium-size onions (chopped), or 2 leeks (shredded)
4 small carrots (cut in julienne strips)
½ head of celery (cut in julienne strips)
3 tomatoes
salt and pepper

The term **julienne** can mean either a clear vegetable soup (consommé julienne) to which a mixture of finely shredded, cooked vegetables has been added, or indicate the cut size and shape of vegetables and garnishes for certain dishes. A julienne strip is usually about ⅛ inch by 1½-2 inches long.

Method

Prepare sweetbreads as directed on page 56.

Set oven at 375°F or Mark 5. Brown breads lightly in hot butter in a casserole, take out and keep warm. Mix flour with the butter in casserole, then add the stock, purée and seasoning ; stir until boiling. Put back the sweetbreads, check seasoning, cover and cook in pre-set oven for 40-50 minutes or until very tender.

Meanwhile prepare a julienne (garnish of vegetables). Melt the butter in a small shallow pan or casserole, add the onion, carrots and celery, cover tightly and cook gently on top of the stove for 5 minutes, then put in the oven for a further 10-15 minutes. Skin the tomatoes, quarter, remove seeds ; add with seasoning to the other vegetables and cook for a further 2-3 minutes.

Take up the sweetbreads, reduce sauce and skim well ; add shredded ham, parsley and cream.

Place sweetbreads on the julienne in an ovenproof dish. Pipe round a border of creamed potatoes. Serve at once or brown in oven before serving ; in the latter case dust a little grated Parmesan cheese over the top.

Vegetable dishes

Many people do not realise that quite ordinary vegetables can be turned into excellent lunch or supper dishes. A well cooked vegetable can also be eaten as a separate course for a party meal if you want to eat French-style.

This is probably the best way to savour some of the more unusual vegetables, too, and there are many that lend themselves particularly well to casserole cooking and braising — aubergine, for instance, needs very thorough cooking or it will be indigestible, and what better way to do this than in a casserole ?

Dried vegetables, too, need prolonged soaking and cooking to make them tender. So casserole or braise them with an inexpensive cut of belly pork, mutton, or sausage, for a tasty, nourishing dish.

Dried vegetables should be chosen carefully and should not be more than one year old. After this they become hard and no amount of soaking and cooking will make them really tender. To prepare them, wash the vegetables and pick them over to remove any grit or small stones. Soak them in tepid water (plenty of it) for 8 hours, or leave overnight. If they have to be left longer, change the water or they may start to ferment.

Then drain the vegetables, cover with plenty of fresh, warm water and cook in a covered pan. If the water is hard, add a pinch of bicarbonate of soda which will help to soften the outer skins. Salt is never added at this stage as it would harden them. Bring them very slowly to boiling point, allowing 30-40 minutes, then simmer gently for about 1 hour. Drain them again and then use as specified.

In this section we have also included casseroles that contain meat with a large proportion of vegetables.

Casserole of potatoes and mushrooms

1 ½ lb even-size potatoes, or 1 lb
   new potatoes
8 oz button mushrooms
1 oz butter
2 tablespoons plain flour
1 pint milk, or ½ pint milk and
   ½ pint potato water
salt and pepper
1-2 tablespoons double cream
   (or milk and potato water)
pinch of grated nutmeg

Method
Peel potatoes and cut each one in four. (If using new ones, leave them whole.) Trim the cut edges with a potato peeler. Cook carefully in salted water until barely tender. Tip away water (if not using), dry over gentle heat. Cover and set aside.

Wash the mushrooms in salted water and trim the stalks.
Watchpoint Be careful not to pull out the stalks or the mushrooms will shrink during cooking. The stalk keeps the mushroom in shape.

Melt the butter and toss mushrooms in it over a high heat. Mix in the flour, milk (or milk and potato water) and seasoning and stir until boiling. Add the potatoes, cover the pan and simmer for 10 minutes. Stir in cream and a pinch of grated nutmeg.
Note : this dish is best done with tiny, new potatoes but canned new ones will do. In this case, follow the instructions for heating on the can. Drain and put them into the sauce. Do not simmer for 10 minutes as with fresh potatoes, but finish off immediately with the cream and nutmeg and keep warm.

Chilli con carne

6 oz red beans (soaked and
   pre-cooked — see page 65)
1 lb minced steak
2 tablespoons oil, or dripping
2 onions (finely chopped)
2 tablespoons chilli con carne spice,
   or 1 dessertspoon chilli powder
1 dessertspoon paprika pepper
about ½ pint of water

Method
Choose a large stew pan or deep frying pan, heat the dripping in this, add onion and when it is about to turn colour, add the spices. Add the mince, stirring for 4-5 minutes, then add the drained beans and a little of their cooking liquor.

Cover and simmer until beef and beans are tender (about 1½ hours). During this time the pan should be covered and if the mixture gets too thick add a little of the water. The consistency should be that of a rich stew.

Cassoulet

1 lb haricot beans (soaked and pre-cooked as directed on page 65)
6 oz salt belly pork, or green streaky bacon
4 cloves of garlic (finely chopped)
$\frac{1}{2}$ shoulder of mutton, or half a duck
2 tablespoons good beef dripping, or bacon fat, or butter
bouquet garni
salt and black pepper
4 oz garlic, or pork, sausage
$\frac{3}{4}$ lb ripe tomatoes, or 1 medium-size can
1 dessertspoon tomato purée
1 teaspoon sugar
browned breadcrumbs (see page 136)

This is a traditional dish from the Languedoc region of France and it contains many specialities of that region. The following recipe is simplified with mutton to replace the traditional pickled goose. If preferred, half a duck could be used. Garlic sausage can be obtained at most delicatessens, or you can use a pork sausage.

Method

Drain the beans and put into a large flameproof casserole with the pork or bacon and the finely chopped garlic. Pour in water to cover well, put on lid, simmer gently 1-1$\frac{1}{4}$ hours. Drain, set aside and reserve liquor.

Bone the mutton and cut into large cubes or leave the duck in one piece. Fry until golden-brown in the dripping, add the beans and pork to the casserole with the herbs and a little salt, and a lot of black pepper. Moisten with some of the bean liquor, cover and stew very slowly for 3-4 hours, adding a little more of the cooking liquor from time to time, if necessary. After 2$\frac{1}{2}$ hours' cooking, add the garlic sausage. When the beans are tender, take out pork, remove skin and slice ; also slice the sausage ; replace pork (or bacon) and sausage in casserole.

Cook the tomatoes to a pulp in a separate pan, add the tomato purée and season with salt, pepper and sugar. Spoon this mixture over the beans, shake the casserole gently to mix it in, then sprinkle the top of the beans with the browned crumbs. Put in hot oven, pre-set at 375°F or Mark 5, for$\frac{3}{4}$-1 hour to brown.

Casserole of salsify

1½ lb salsify (scorzonera, or white)
1 oz butter
1 medium-size onion (chopped)
2 oz mushrooms (sliced)
1 dessertspoon plain flour
1 wineglass white wine
½ pint stock (see page 134)
salt and pepper
½ lb tomatoes, or 1 cup canned
   tomatoes
1 tablespoon freshly chopped herbs,
   or parsley
Parmesan cheese (grated) — for
   serving

Method

To prepare salsify : scrub the roots well and if necessary cut salsify into 3-4 inch lengths. Boil the salsify until tender (about 40 minutes) then drain and peel off the thick black skin. Melt the butter in a flameproof casserole, add onion and, after a few minutes, the mushrooms. Cook for 3 minutes, then stir in flour ; add wine and stock. Season, bring to the boil and simmer for 7-8 minutes. Then add salsify, the tomatoes (skinned, seeds removed, and chopped) and herbs. Simmer for 5 minutes, then serve with a separate dish of grated Parmesan cheese.

Cabbage stuffed with chestnuts

1 firm green cabbage
1 lb chestnuts
1 onion (sliced)
1 oz butter
1¼ pint jellied stock (see page 134)
about ¼ pint brown sauce (see
   page 84)

Method

Trim the cabbage, removing any damaged outside leaves, and plunge in boiling salted water for 5 minutes, tip into a colander and refresh with cold water. Put chestnuts in a pan of cold water, bring to the boil, drain. Remove the inner and outer shell of the chestnuts and put the nuts in a pan with the onion, butter and 1 pint of jellied stock ; cover and cook gently until the chestnuts are tender and the stock has evaporated.

Meanwhile set the oven at 350°F or Mark 4.

Curl back the outer leaves of the cabbage, scoop out the centre and fill with the chestnuts. Reshape the cabbage and fit it into a buttered casserole, pour over ¼ pint of the stock, cover and cook in pre-set moderate oven for 45-50 minutes. Spoon over the brown sauce and return to the oven for 5-10 minutes.

Onion ragoût
(stew)

1 lb button onions, or shallots
1 oz butter
1 teaspoon sugar
1 wineglass white wine, cider, or
   stock (see page 134)

Method
Set oven at 350°F or Mark 4.
   Peel onions, blanch by putting
in pan of cold water and bringing to boil. Drain and turn into
a casserole, add butter, sugar
and wine, or cider, or stock.
Cover tightly, cook until tender
(40-45 minutes) in pre-set oven.
Serve in the casserole.

Casserole of aubergines

4 aubergines (sliced)
salt
oil (for frying)
1 can (5-6 fl oz) vegetable, or
   tomato, sauce
2 cartons of plain yoghourt
black pepper (ground from mill)

Serve with grills or sauté slices
of liver.

Method
Score the sliced aubergines
lightly with a knife, sprinkle
with salt and leave for 30
minutes. Set the oven at 350°F
or Mark 4. Dry the aubergine
slices, heat the oil and fry
aubergine until golden brown
on each side. Put the slices as
they come from the pan into a
casserole, layering them with
the vegetable sauce and yoghourt, season with black pepper. Cover and bake in the pre-
set moderate oven for about 40
minutes. Turn out for serving.

Haricot beans with sausages

½ lb haricot beans (soaked and
   pre-cooked — see page 65)
1 lb pork sausages
1 oz butter
1 medium-size onion (finely
   chopped)
1 dessertspoon plain flour
2 tablespoons stock (see page 134)
1 wineglass white wine
salt and pepper
squeeze of lemon juice
½ oz butter

Method
Fry the sausages until cooked
and brown on all sides, then add
the beans and cook until they
are slightly browned and have
absorbed the fat from the
sausages ; turn them into a
casserole.
   Melt the butter, add the onion
and cook until brown ; stir in
the flour, stock and wine,
season and bring to the boil.
Cook for 10 minutes, add a
squeeze of lemon juice and
pour over the beans and sausages. Dot the butter over the
beans and shake well until
absorbed. Serve very hot and
well seasoned.

Puchero bean stew
(with pork and tomatoes)

$\frac{1}{2}$ lb red, or brown, beans (soaked overnight in plenty of water)
1 lb salt belly of pork (or beef flank, or brisket)
2 tablespoons salad oil
1 large onion (peeled and sliced)
1 large carrot (peeled and sliced)
1-2 cloves of garlic (chopped)
1 dessertspoon tomato purée
1-1$\frac{1}{2}$ pints stock (see page 134), or water
pepper
bouquet garni
2 caps of pimiento (sliced)
$\frac{1}{2}$ lb ripe tomatoes (skinned and halved)
2 saveloys, or equivalent in smoked sausage (about 6 oz)

Puchero (a stew) is a dish of Spanish origin, and there are several versions but this particular recipe comes from South America.

Method

Drain beans, put into a large pan, well cover with cold water and bring slowly to the boil. Simmer for 1$\frac{1}{2}$ hours.

Meanwhile put the meat in a separate pan of cold water, bring to the boil and continue cooking for about 1 hour. Then drain both the beans and meat.

Heat oil in the pan in which the beans were cooked, add onion and carrot slices and garlic. Cook for 4-5 minutes, then add beans, tomato purée and stock (or water). Add a little pepper but no salt. Bring pan to the boil, put in the meat, add the bouquet garni, cover and simmer until beans and meat are tender (about 1$\frac{1}{2}$ hours). After 1 hour add the prepared pimiento and tomatoes.

Blanch sausages by putting in cold water, bringing to boil and draining. Then add to the stew and continue to simmer. The puchero should be thick and rich by this time ; if too thick, add a little extra stock, or water.

Before dishing up, take out meat and sausages and slice them. Return slices to the puchero. Adjust seasoning and turn the stew into a deep serving dish or casserole.

Ratatouille

½ lb courgettes
1-2 aubergines
½ lb, or 1 medium-size can, tomatoes
1 large green pepper
1 large red pepper
2 small onions (finely sliced into rings)
2 cloves of garlic (chopped) — optional
4 tablespoons olive oil
salt and pepper

Method

Slice, and salt the courgettes and aubergines and set aside. Scald, skin and remove seeds of fresh tomatoes and slice roughly, or drain canned ones. Halve the peppers, removing core and seeds, and cut into fine shreds.

Heat the oil in a stewpan, and fry the onion rings and garlic for 2-3 minutes. Wipe dry the courgettes and aubergines, add them to the pan and fry for 2-3 minutes on each side, adding extra oil as needed. Season the mixture, add shredded peppers and tomatoes, cover the pan and cook gently for a good hour or more on top of the stove, or in the oven at 350°F or Mark 4. The ratatouille should cook down to a soft, rich mass.

Boston baked beans

1 lb dried pea beans
2 pints water
2 teaspoons dry mustard
¼ teaspoon black, or white, pepper
1 tablespoon salt
3 medium-size onions
1 tablespoon black treacle
1 tablespoon golden syrup
2 oz soft brown sugar
½ lb salt belly pork

Method

Pick over and wash the beans in several changes of water, then soak overnight in 1 pint of the measured water.

Set the oven at 250°F or Mark ½. Mix the mustard, pepper and salt with 1 pint water in a large casserole and tip in the beans with their soaking liquor. Quarter the onions and add to the casserole with the treacle, syrup and brown sugar. Cover and put in pre-set slow oven to bake for 6-8 hours.

Soak the pork in cold water for 1 hour, then blanch for 10 minutes. Remove the skin, cut into lardons, add to casserole and continue cooking for about 1 hour or until the meat is very tender.

If necessary, add extra water at the same time as the pork. Remove the lid of casserole for last 30 minutes.

Right : Boston baked beans with lardons of salt belly pork, casseroled

Adding onions to soaked pea beans with treacle, syrup and brown sugar

Removing the skin from salt belly pork after soaking and blanching it

Dolmas

1 green cabbage

For filling
4 rounded tablespoons rice (cooked)
1 medium-size onion (finely chopped)
1 oz butter
4 oz mushrooms
2 hard-boiled eggs
1 dessertspoon plain flour
$\frac{1}{2}$ pint vegetable stock (see page 134)
1 dessertspoon tomato purée, or
   1 tablespoon canned tomatoes
kneaded butter (see page 141)
$\frac{1}{2}$ lb tomatoes

Method

Boil rice for 10-12 minutes, or until tender, in plenty of boiling salted water. Strain, rinse and strain again. Put on one side.

Wash cabbage, trim off stalk. Put into a large pan of boiling salted water and boil gently for 3-4 minutes. Lift out and begin peeling off the leaves. As soon as they become difficult to detach, put cabbage back into the boiling water to make the remainder soft and easy to remove. When all the leaves are detached, apart from the heart, prepare the filling.

To make filling : soften the onion in butter, add mushrooms, washed and finely chopped. Turn into a bowl and mix with the cooked rice and the hard-boiled eggs, finely chopped. Now snip out the cabbage stalk in each leaf with scissors. Place 1 dessertspoon of the mixture on each leaf and roll up like a small parcel. Roll each one lightly in flour, pack into a deep fireproof dish or pan.

Watchpoint Arrange each dolma at an angle so that it does not come into close contact with the others.

Pour over enough stock just to cover, bring to the boil, put on the lid, or cover with buttered paper, and simmer for about 45 minutes either on top of the stove or inside the oven at 325°F or Mark 3. Then tip stock into a pan, add either canned tomatoes or tomato purée, thicken with a little kneaded butter and boil again. Now peel fresh tomatoes, quarter and flick out seeds, then cut each quarter into three, lengthways. Arrange the dolmas in a serving dish or leave in the pan. Add tomato pieces to sauce and spoon over the dish.

1
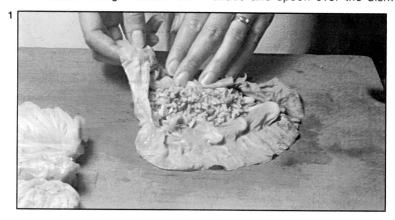

1 How to stuff cabbage leaves for dolmas. Take a softened leaf and spoon a little of the savoury filling into the centre

2 Fold leaf corners into the centre and roll up like a small parcel. Repeat this until all leaves are used

3 Then roll each of the finished leaves in a little flour ready for cooking

75

Braised cabbage

1 firm white cabbage
1 large onion (sliced)
1 oz butter
1 cooking apple (peeled and sliced)
salt and pepper
1-2 tablespoons stock (see page 134)

Method

Cut the cabbage in quarters and cut away the core. Shred finely. If you are using hard white Dutch cabbage, blanch by putting into boiling, salted water for 1 minute, draining and refreshing with 1 cup of cold water. This is not necessary for green cabbage. Slice the onion and put in a flameproof casserole with the butter. Cook over gentle heat until soft but not coloured. Add the cabbage to the pan with the peeled and sliced apple. Season, stir well and pour in the stock. Cover with non-stick (silicone) cooking paper and lid, and cook for 45-50 minutes on the bottom shelf of the oven, pre-set at 325°F or Mark 3.

Cabbage alsacienne

1 white Dutch cabbage (shredded)
1 oz butter
1 small head of celery (shredded)
1 wineglass dry white wine, or same quantity of stock (see page 134) with 1 teaspoon wine vinegar
salt and pepper
1 tablespoon chopped parsley

Method

Blanch cabbage in pan of boiling salted water for 1 minute, then drain well.

Melt butter in a shallow pan or casserole, add celery and cook for 2-3 minutes. Add the cabbage and wine, or stock and wine vinegar. Season well, cover and cook gently for 25-30 minutes. Sprinkle with chopped parsley before serving.

Potato goulash

1½ lb small new potatoes
1 tablespoon oil, or lard
½ lb onions (finely chopped)
¼ clove of garlic (finely chopped)
1 dessertspoon paprika pepper
1 dessertspoon plain flour
2 tablespoons wine vinegar
¼-½ pint stock (see page 134), or
  water
salt and pepper
½ teaspoon caraway seeds
  (optional)
1 green pepper (sliced and
  blanched)
2 tomatoes (skinned, seeds
  removed, shredded)
2 tablespoons yoghourt, or soured,
  or fresh, cream

Method
Cook the potatoes in boiling salted water for 15 minutes. Meanwhile heat the oil (or lard) in a flameproof casserole, add the onions and garlic and cook slowly until golden-brown, stir in the paprika pepper and continue cooking for 1 minute. Remove from heat, blend in flour, vinegar and stock (or water). Season, bring to boil.

Drain the potatoes and put in the casserole with the caraway seeds (if used), green pepper and tomatoes ; cook for 5-10 minutes until potatoes are tender.

Just before serving, spoon the yoghourt or cream over the potatoes ; shake pan gently to blend cream with the sauce.

Braised celery

3 large sticks of celery
1 large onion (diced)
1 large carrot (diced)
1 oz butter
½ pint jellied stock (see page 134)
salt and pepper
bouquet garni

Method
Wash celery, split sticks in two, blanch in boiling, salted water and drain.

Dice the onion and carrot, sweat them in butter in a pan. Then add the celery, stock, seasoning and bouquet garni. Cover and braise for 1-1½ hours, or until tender, in an oven at 325°F or Mark 3. Baste well from time to time.

When cooked, the gravy should be well reduced and the celery glazed. Dish up and strain gravy over the celery.

Braised chicory

6-8 pieces of chicory
1 oz butter
juice of ½ lemon
½ teaspoon salt (dissolved in
  1 tablespoon water)
black pepper (ground from mill)

Method
Wipe the chicory, remove any marked outside leaves and scoop out the small core at the bottom. Rub the butter round a casserole dish, put in the chicory and pour over it the lemon juice and salt water.

Add a little black pepper, cover with a buttered grease-proof paper and the lid of the casserole and cook for 1 hour in oven at 350°F or Mark 4.

Casserole of onions and potatoes

¾ lb button onions
1 oz butter
1 teaspoon sugar
½ pint stock (see page 134)
1 lb new potatoes (scraped),
 or 1 lb old potatoes (peeled and
 cut into small pieces), or 1 can
 new potatoes
1 teaspoon chopped parsley
 (optional)

Method
Blanch onions by putting in pan of cold water and bringing to boil ; strain before further cooking. Return to a flameproof casserole with butter, sugar and stock. Boil gently until onions are tender and stock has reduced to about 2 tablespoons (about 20-30 minutes). Do not allow onions to brown.

Cook potatoes in boiling salted water, or heat canned ones. Drain and add to the onions with parsley. Serve in the casserole.

Potatoes with onions cooked in butter, and stock, make a good casserole

Poultry dishes

To catch a bird and pop it in the pot is one of the oldest ways of producing a first class meal.

Chicken, duck, goose and turkey are all good for casseroles and braises. You can leave the bird whole for braising, and either carve or joint it for serving ; for casseroles it is usual to joint it before cooking. The diagrams and photographs below and on page 80 show how to joint a small duck and a chicken.

Jointing a small duck

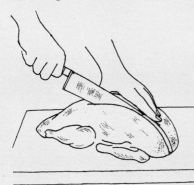 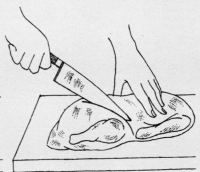

First set duck on a board and cut down through the breastbone and back. Scissors are best for cutting through the bone ; use a knife for the flesh

Lay each half on the board and make a slanting cut between ribs to separate the wing and leg ; this gives you four portions. Trim away the bone

Jointing a fresh chicken

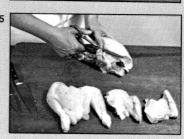

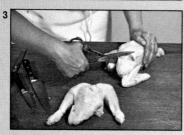

1 Hold chicken firmly on board with one hand. With sharp knife, saw away skin between leg and breast. Then, pressing flat of knife against carcass, take leg in other hand and bend it outwards until oyster bone breaks away from carcass

2 Slide the knife around the leg joint cutting down towards the 'parson's nose', keeping it between the oyster and backbone. Leg is now severed from the carcass and has the oyster bone attached. Cut off the other leg in the same way

3 Now make a slantwise cut with knife half-way up the breast across to the top of wishbone from the neck end, to end of the wing joints. With scissors, cut down through wishbone and ribs to detach the wing with a good portion of breast

4 Twist the wing pinion out and tuck it under this breast meat to hold the joint flat. This makes for even browning of the meat. To get both wings of even size, make the slantwise cuts at the same time. Detach other wing in the same way

5 Cut away the breast meat in one piece with the scissors. All that is now left of the carcass are the ribs, the backbone and the 'parson's nose'

6 The joints are now ready for cooking. The carcass may be cut in half and then sautéd with the chicken joints to give the finished dish additional flavour

Braised duckling with olives

1 duckling
1 oz butter
1 medium-size onion (sliced)
1 glass port
1 teaspoon paprika pepper
½ pint jellied stock (see page 134)
bouquet garni
salt and pepper
2 tomatoes
12 large green olives, or olives
   stuffed with pimiento
1 dessertspoon plain flour

Method

Brown the duckling in butter in a deep flameproof casserole; when evenly coloured, tip off the fat and add the onion; cover and cook slowly until the onion is soft.

Moisten bird with the port; allow liquid to reduce by half and then stir in the paprika and cook for 2-3 minutes. Pour on the stock, add the bouquet garni and season lightly. Cover casserole and cook very gently for about 45 minutes or until duckling is tender. This cooking can be done on top of the stove, or in the oven at 350°F or Mark 4.

Meanwhile skin and quarter the tomatoes, remove the seeds, then cut the flesh into neat shreds. Set aside.

If using large olives, cut in strips off the stones; if using stuffed olives, leave them whole, blanch in boiling water for 5 minutes, drain and leave to soak in cold water for 30 minutes, then drain again.

Remove the duckling from the casserole and keep hot; take out the bouquet garni. Skim the fat from the liquid in casserole. Mix the flour with 1 tablespoon of the liquid, return this to the casserole and stir until it boils. Cook liquid for 5 minutes. Add the tomatoes and olives, reheat and taste for seasoning.

Divide the duckling into four portions, place them in a hot serving dish and spoon over the sauce. Serve with beans, peas and very tiny roast potatoes.

Salmis of duck

1 duckling
1 oz butter
1 shallot (finely chopped)
$\frac{3}{4}$ oz plain flour
$\frac{3}{4}$ pint white bone, or chicken, stock (see page 134)
1 wineglass dry white wine
salt and pepper
bouquet garni

For garnish
8-10 green olives (stoned)
8-10 chipolata sausages
6-8 croûtes of bread (fried in butter)

Salmis is the name given to a brown ragoût of duck or game. The bird is lightly roasted before being split, jointed or carved and then put in a rich brown sauce flavoured with wine. Further cooking is then done either on top of the stove or in the oven, and the finished dish is garnished with bread croûtes.

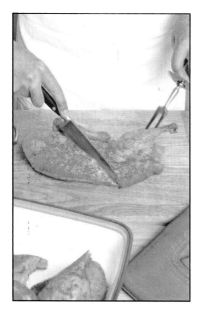

Method

Set oven at 425°F. or Mark 7.

Prick the skin of the duckling all over with a trussing needle (this is to help the fat to run), place in a roasting tin and cook in the pre-set hot oven for 30 minutes. Meanwhile, melt the butter in a large pan, add the shallot and cook gently for 1-2 minutes, then blend in the flour and allow it to colour slowly until it is a good russet-brown. Remove pan from the heat, whisk in $\frac{1}{2}$ pint of stock and the wine, return pan to the heat and stir until boiling. Season, add bouquet garni and simmer for 20 minutes.

Tip half the remaining cold stock into the pan, bring to the boil and then skim sauce well. Repeat this process and continue simmering it gently while the duckling is roasting. Take up the duck, joint it and set portions in a shallow ovenproof casserole ; spoon over the sauce and cover with a lid. Turn the oven to 350°F or Mark 4, put in the duck and continue cooking for about 20 minutes.

To prepare garnish : leave the olives to soak in hot water ; grill or fry the sausages. For serving, remove the lid of the casserole, garnish the duck with the sausages and drained olives and arrange the fried croûtes around. Serve with new potatoes and minted peas.

82

Left : carving duckling in portions

*Left : adding croûtes to the salmis
Below : the finished salmis of duck*

Braised goose (or capon)

1 young, tender ('green') goose, or capon — 5-6 lb

For farce
1 lb minced pork, or sausage meat
1 cup fresh white breadcrumbs
1 dessertspoon dried herbs
1 tablespoon chopped fresh parsley
1 medium-size onion
1 oz butter
salt and pepper
pinch of ground mace
1 egg (beaten)

For braising
little dripping, or butter
2 onions (sliced)
2 carrots (sliced)
1 turnip (diced)
2-3 sticks of celery (sliced)
bouquet garni
6 peppercorns
$\frac{3}{4}$-1 pint good brown stock (see page 134)
1 wineglass red wine

For brown sauce
1 tablespoon each finely diced carrot and onion
1 stick of celery (diced)
1-2 tablespoons dripping
1 tablespoon plain flour
1 teaspoon tomato purée
$\frac{1}{2}$-$\frac{3}{4}$ pint stock
2 wineglasses red wine
little slaked arrowroot (optional)

For garnish
braised chestnuts (see right)
$\frac{1}{2}$-$\frac{3}{4}$ lb chipolata sausages (fried)

Method

Set oven at 350-375°F or Mark 4-5.

To make the farce : mix the meat, crumbs and herbs together in a basin. Chop the onion and cook in a pan with the butter until soft, then add to the mixture. Season well, add mace and bind with the egg.

Stuff the goose with farce and truss. Rub a braising pan, or flameproof casserole, with a little dripping or butter. Put the braising vegetables in this, cover and sweat for 5-7 minutes. Then put the goose on top and the bouquet garni and peppercorns at the side. Add the stock. Raise the heat and allow the liquid to reduce by about a quarter, then add the wine ; cover the bird with a piece of paper and then the lid and cook gently in the pre-set oven for about 2 hours, basting frequently. After about 1$\frac{1}{2}$ hours, remove the lid and continue to cook, basting well and adding a little more stock if necessary, until the goose is nicely crisp.

Meanwhile prepare the brown sauce by cooking the diced vegetables in 1-2 tablespoons of dripping. When barely coloured, stir in the flour and continue to cook to a russet-brown. Then draw aside and add the tomato purée and stock. Bring to the boil and simmer, with the pan half covered, for about 30 minutes. Then add the wine and continue to cook uncovered for a further 20 minutes. Strain, rinse out the pan and return the sauce to it ; set aside.

Take up the goose, place it on a large meat dish and keep warm. Strain off the liquid and skim thoroughly to remove the fat. Add the liquid to the brown sauce, then boil gently, to reduce, until it has a good flavour (5-6 minutes). Thicken if necessary with arrowroot slaked in a little cold water. Pour a little of this sauce round the goose and surround with the garnish of fried chipolata sausages and braised chestnuts. Serve remaining sauce in a sauce boat.

Braised chestnuts
Put 1 lb chestnuts in a pan, cover them with cold water and bring to the boil. Draw pan aside ; take out the nuts one at a time and strip off the outer and inner skin. When all the nuts are skinned, put them in a stew pan, cover with about $\frac{3}{4}$ pint jellied stock, season lightly, put the lid on the pan and simmer until the nuts are tender (about 20-30 minutes). Then take off the lid and increase the heat to reduce any remaining stock. The nuts should be nicely glazed.

Mexican chicken

4-6 chicken leg joints
2 teaspoons chilli con carne
   spice, or chilli powder
1 teaspoon plain flour
2 tablespoons olive oil
1 large onion (finely chopped)
1 can, or 1 lb, tomatoes
   (skinned, sliced and seeds
   removed)
1 clove of garlic (crushed with salt)
bouquet garni

Method
Roll the chicken joints in a mixture of the spice and flour and set aside. Heat the oil in a casserole, add the onion and cook until golden, then add the chicken and colour slowly on all sides. Tip on the tomatoes, add the garlic and the herbs and bring to the boil. Simmer gently for about 40 minutes, or until tender ; serve with risi-bisi.

Risi-bisi

5-6 oz rice
salt and pepper
2 oz butter
1 packet (6-8 oz) frozen peas
   (cooked)

Method
Cook the rice in plenty of boiling salted water until tender, drain well and dry.
   Melt the butter in a large sauté pan, add the rice and toss carefully with a fork until really hot. Season and add the cooked peas.

Coq au vin

3 ½-4 lb roasting chicken
4 oz gammon rashers
4 oz button onions
2 oz butter
¼ bottle of Burgundy (7 fl oz)
2 cloves of garlic (crushed with
  ½ teaspoon salt)
bouquet garni
¼-½ pint chicken stock (see page 134)
salt and pepper
kneaded butter

For garnish
1 French roll (for croûtes) — sliced
butter, or salad oil (for frying)
chopped parsley

If good wine has been used for this dish it needs no accompanying vegetable except creamed potatoes ; anything else detracts from the flavour of the sauce.

Joint the chicken after it has been browned in butter ; the chicken, below, has had one leg removed, the other one is being taken off

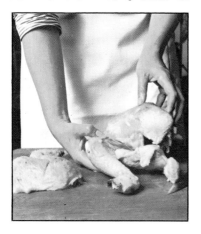

Method

First truss the chicken or tie neatly. This is important even though the bird is jointed immediately after browning as it stays compact, making it easy to turn in casserole during browning.

Remove rind and rust from the bacon, cut into lardons (¼-inch thick strips, 1½ inches long). Blanch these and onions by putting into a pan of cold water, bringing to the boil and draining well.

Brown chicken slowly in butter, then remove from casserole. Add onions and lardons ; while these are browning, joint chicken. Replace joints in casserole pan and 'flame' by pouring on wine and setting it alight. Add the crushed garlic, bouquet garni, stock and seasoning. Cover casserole and cook slowly for about 1 hour, either on top of stove, or in pre-set oven at 325°F or Mark 3.

To make croûtes : fry slices of bread on both sides in butter or oil until golden-brown.

Test to see if chicken is tender by piercing flesh of the thigh with a fine-pointed cooking knife. If clear liquid runs out, it is ready ; if pink, continue cooking. When ready remove chicken and bouquet garni and taste sauce for seasoning. Thicken slightly with kneaded butter, then dish up chicken in casserole with sauce. Surround with croûtes and sprinkle with chopped parsley. Serve with creamed potatoes (see page 30).

The finished coq au vin ready to serve

Chicken Paulette

2½-3 lb roasting chicken
(jointed), or 5-6 chicken joints
1 tablespoon olive oil
1 oz butter

For mirepoix
8 spring onions
1 carrot
3 mushrooms
pinch of saffron
pinch of ground ginger
1 glass sherry
¼ pint stock (made from giblets - see page 134)
1 teaspoon arrowroot (slaked with 1 tablespoon cold water)
¼ pint double cream
1 tablespoon French mustard (preferably Grey Poupon)

Method
Brown the chicken joints in the hot oil and butter in a flame-proof casserole, then take them out and set aside.

To prepare mirepoix : trim and cut the spring onions into ½-inch pieces, dice the carrot and chop the mushrooms. Put these vegetables into the same casserole as used before, cover and cook gently for 4-5 minutes, then replace the pieces of chicken, add the spices, sherry and stock, cover pan, or casserole, and cook gently for 30-40 minutes. Dish up the pieces of chicken and keep them warm.

Boil the sauce for 2-3 minutes. Thicken it with the arrowroot, then add the cream and mustard. Boil up sauce, taste for seasoning and spoon it over the chicken. Serve at once.

Tandoori chicken

2 lb roasting chicken
1 large onion
2-3 cloves of garlic
1-inch piece of fresh ginger
1 teaspoon coriander powder
1 teaspoon cumin powder
¼ teaspoon chilli powder
1½ teaspoons salt
1 carton (5 fl oz) plain yoghourt
2 teaspoons vinegar
2 teaspoons Worcestershire sauce
juice of 2 small lemons
1½ oz butter
1 teaspoon garam masala (see right)

A tandoori oven is an earthenware pot into which hot charcoal is put before burying it in the earth. When the pot is thoroughly hot the charcoal is removed and the chicken cooked in the pot by the retained heat.

You can cook this dish in an ordinary oven or on a rotary spit.

Method
Make three or four cuts on the side and legs of the bird. Finely mince the onion, garlic and ginger to a paste, add the coriander, cumin, chilli and salt. Beat the yoghourt into vinegar and Worcestershire sauce, add the juice of 1 lemon ; mix thoroughly with the spices. Rub this into the cuts in the bird and leave for about 6 hours.

Set the oven at 325°F or Mark 3. Melt 1 oz butter in a casserole and cook the chicken with the lid on for about 40 minutes, or until tender, in the pre-set oven. To serve, joint the bird, brush with remaining butter (melted), sprinkle with garam masala and the rest of the lemon juice.

Chicken casserole with peaches

3 lb roasting chicken
2 large onions
3 oz butter
2-3 peaches (peeled and sliced)
— preferably Hale
pinch of nutmeg
rind and juice of 1 lemon
$\frac{1}{2}$ pint chicken stock (see page 134)
salt
black pepper (ground from mill)
3-4 tablespoons double cream
paprika pepper

For pilaf
1-2 oz onions (chopped)
1 oz butter
8 oz long grain rice
1 dessertspoon turmeric
1-1$\frac{1}{4}$ pints chicken stock, or water

Method

Joint the chicken neatly a few hours before cooking, so that the back and trimmings can be made into stock.

Finely slice the onions. Fry the chicken slowly to a golden-brown in half the butter. Melt the remaining butter in a flame-proof casserole, fry the onions slowly and, when turning colour, add the peaches ; continue frying over quicker heat for a few more minutes.

Put the chicken joints into the casserole with the onions and peaches. Add nutmeg with two strips of pared lemon rind ; then add the stock and seasoning. Cover the casserole tightly and stew chicken slowly in moderate oven pre-set at 350°F or Mark 4 for about 1 hour.

Meanwhile prepare the pilaf. Chop the onions and soften them in the butter in a flame-proof casserole. Add the rice and turmeric and fry together. Pour on the stock (or water), season well, bring to the boil, cover, and cook in the oven until the rice is tender and the stock absorbed.

When the chicken is very tender, remove it and the lemon rind from the pan. Boil up the juices in the pan, adding lemon juice to taste, and adjust the seasoning. Stir in the cream and boil sauce rapidly until it coats the back of a spoon.

Dish up the chicken, pour over the sauce, dust with paprika pepper and serve the pilaf separately.

Garam masala

$\frac{3}{4}$ oz cinnamon
$\frac{1}{4}$ oz cloves
$\frac{3}{4}$ oz brown cardamom seeds
$\frac{1}{4}$ oz black cumin seeds
good pinch of mace
good pinch of nutmeg

Method

Grind ingredients together, or pound in a mortar, then pass through a fine sieve. This will keep up to two weeks in an airtight container.

Curried chicken with peaches

3½ lb roasting chicken
2 tablespoons olive oil, or butter
1 medium-size onion (finely chopped)
1 rounded tablespoon curry powder
1 rounded tablespoon plain flour
¾ pint chicken stock (made from the giblets — see page 134)
1 clove of garlic (crushed with ½ teaspoon salt)
¼ pint nut milk (see box)
1 tablespoon redcurrant jelly, or juice of ½ lemon mixed with 1 dessertspoon sugar
3-4 tablespoons double cream
1 teaspoon arrowroot (optional)
2 fresh white-fleshed peaches (peeled and sliced)

To serve
8 oz rice (boiled) — see page 139

Method

Joint the chicken, leaving plenty of carcass bone to prevent the flesh shrinking, and brown it slowly in half the oil (or butter) in a flameproof casserole. Remove chicken joints from the casserole and keep warm.

Heat the remaining oil (or butter), add the onion and cook gently until it is just turning colour. Stir in the curry powder and continue cooking for 2-3 minutes. Dust in the flour and cook for 1 minute. Draw casserole away from the heat and gradually add the stock, then stir in the garlic and allow to simmer for 20 minutes. Put the chicken back in the casserole, cover tightly and continue cooking on top of the stove or in the oven, pre-set at 325°F or Mark 3, for about 45 minutes until tender. Trim the chicken joints and strain the sauce from the casserole into a pan. Add the nut milk with the redcurrant jelly (or lemon juice and sugar) to sauce, simmer it for 2-3 minutes.

Wipe out the casserole and replace the chicken. Add the cream to the sauce and thicken, if necessary, with arrowroot slaked with a little stock or water. Spoon curry sauce over the chicken and reheat carefully. About 10-15 minutes before serving, add peaches. Serve boiled rice separately.

> **Nut milk.** To make ¼ pint of this milk, infuse 2 tablespoons ground almonds or desiccated coconut in 1 teacup of boiling water for 1 hour. Then strain liquid before use.

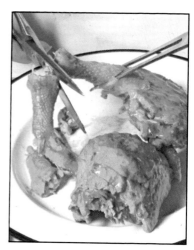

*Above : trimming the casseroled chicken joints before adding sauce
Right : curried chicken is delicious with fresh peaches added to sauce*

Chicken waterzoi

1 roasting chicken (weighing 3 lb)
3 young carrots
1 medium-size onion
2 leeks
1 oz butter
salt and pepper
pinch of sugar
2 wineglasses white wine
4 parsley roots (Hamburg
  parsley if possible)
$\frac{1}{2}$-$\frac{3}{4}$ pint chicken stock (see page 134)
2 teaspoons arrowroot
2 egg yolks
3-4 fl oz double cream
chopped chervil and tarragon

This dish is Flemish in origin
and the name is derived from
waterzootje, which is in fact
a fish dish, but chicken waterzoi
is prepared in the same way.

Method

Set oven at 350°F or Mark 4.

Cut the vegetables in julienne
strips (see page 64). Melt half
the butter in a small flameproof
pan and add the vegetables ;
cover and cook for 1 minute,
then season lightly and add
the sugar. Pour over 1 glass
of wine and bring to the boil ;
cover with a buttered paper and
lid and cook in pre-set moderate
oven until the wine has evaporated (about 10 minutes).

Wash and scrape the parsley
roots well and tie them together
with string. Season inside the
bird with salt and pepper and
truss neatly. Rub the remaining
butter round the sides of a deep
flameproof casserole, put in the
chicken, pour over the rest of
the wine and the stock and set
the parsley roots alongside.
Season with salt and pepper
and scatter the vegetables over
the chicken ; cover with a
buttered paper and close-
fitting lid and bring to the boil.
Turn the oven down to 325°F
or Mark 3 and cook the chicken
until it is very tender (about
1-1$\frac{1}{2}$ hours).

Take up the chicken, cut it
into neat joints and arrange in a
deep serving dish. Lift out the
parsley roots, rub them through
a wire strainer and return this
purée to the casserole. Mix the
arrowroot with the egg yolks and
add the cream ; stir this into the
vegetables and stock and cook
gently until sauce coats a wood-
en spoon. Taste for seasoning,
spoon sauce over chicken.

Sprinkle over a little chopped
chervil and tarragon.

Chicken with tarragon
(Poulet à l'estragon)

3-3½ lb roasting, or boiling, fowl
barding bacon (to cover the breast)
1 onion (sliced)
1 carrot (sliced)
1 stick of celery (sliced)
parsley root, or stalks
1 wineglass white wine
salt

For stock
3 pints water
chicken giblets
1 veal knuckle bone
root vegetables
bouquet garni

For sauce
stock (from the chicken)
good bunch of tarragon
1½ oz butter
½ oz plain flour
3 egg yolks
3 tablespoons double cream
1 tablespoon chopped tarragon
  leaves

Method
First prepare the stock from the giblets and veal bone, allowing it to simmer for about 4 hours, or cut down on this time to about 1 hour by using a pressure cooker.

Bard the breast of the chicken with bacon and sit the bird on the sliced vegetables and parsley in a large saucepan, cover it completely with tepid stock. Then add the wine. Bring to the boil over gentle heat, skim well, add a very little salt and then simmer gently, with the lid half on, for about 1 hour.

Strain off the stock and reserve for the sauce. Keep the chicken hot in the saucepan while making the sauce. Add the tarragon to the stock and boil it hard with the pan uncovered until it is reduced to 1 pint, then strain it. Melt the butter in a pan, stir in the flour off the heat, then add the stock and bring to the boil, stirring all the time ; after the sauce has cooked for 2-3 minutes, add the liaison of egg yolks and cream, then add the chopped tarragon leaves.

Serve the chicken whole or jointed and masked with sauce.

Chicken béarnais

1-2 ½ lb chicken
1-2 oz butter, or bacon fat
1 large onion
4 oz gammon rasher (in the piece)
6-8 baby carrots
1 wineglass white wine, or chicken stock (see page 134)
3 large tomatoes
2 cloves of garlic (crushed with ½ teaspoon salt)
pepper
2 tablespoons double cream (optional)
parsley (chopped) — to garnish

Method

Joint chicken ; when jointing a whole bird for a casserole, put in the back for extra flavour, especially if you have to use water instead of stock.

Set oven at 350°F or Mark 4. Fry joints slowly until golden-brown in the fat, then take out.

Slice onion thinly, cut bacon into squares, blanch both in cold water (bring to boil and drain). Quarter and blanch carrots, lay them in bottom of casserole. Arrange chicken on top, together with onion and bacon. Moisten with wine, or stock, season lightly, cover and cook gently for 1 hour in pre-set oven.

Skin and slice tomatoes, flick out seeds, add flesh to casserole with garlic and pepper. Cover, replace in oven. Continue to cook for 15 minutes or until chicken and carrots are tender. Take out the back of chicken before serving.

Finish, if wished, with the thick cream poured over top just before serving. Dust with chopped parsley.

Chicken à la suisse

3 ½ lb roasting chicken
4 thin rashers of streaky bacon
1 large onion (thinly sliced)
2 large carrots (thinly sliced)
1 stick of celery (sliced)
2 ½ fl oz stock (made from chicken giblets — see page 134)
bouquet garni
½ lb noodles
1 oz butter
pepper (ground from mill)
½ oz Parmesan cheese (grated)

For cheese sauce
1 oz butter
1 oz plain flour
¾ pint milk (infused with 1 slice of onion, 1 bayleaf, 6 pepper-corns, 1 blade of mace)
2 oz Emmenthal, or Gruyère, cheese (grated)
salt and pepper
2-3 tablespoons double cream

Method

Lay the bacon on the bottom of a deep pan, cover with the onion, carrot and celery and set the trussed chicken on top. Cover the pan and cook over very gentle heat for 10-15 minutes. Pour the stock over the

Below : the noodles are tossed in black pepper and butter for chicken à la suisse (see finished dish, right)

chicken, tuck in the bouquet garni with the vegetables, cover again and cook gently, either on top of the stove or in the oven at 325-350°F or Mark 3-4, for about 50-60 minutes.

Meanwhile curl the noodles into a large pan of boiling salted water, reduce the heat a little and boil until just tender ; drain, refresh and put back into the rinsed pan with $\frac{1}{2}$ pint hand-hot water.

Prepare sauce as for a béchamel (see method, page 136) then beat in the grated Emmenthal (or Gruyère) a little at a time and taste for seasoning. Add the cream and keep the sauce warm.

Take up the chicken, reduce the gravy a little and strain. Skim off as much fat as possible, then add the liquid to the cheese sauce. Drain the noodles and heat them in the butter, adding plenty of pepper from the mill before tipping into a hot flameproof serving dish. Carve the chicken, arrange joints on top of the noodles and coat with the sauce. Dust with the grated Parmesan and brown lightly under the grill.

Chicken Majorca

1 roasting chicken (2½-2¾ lb dressed weight)
2 tablespoons olive oil
½ oz butter
1 medium-size onion (thinly sliced)
1 dessertspoon plain flour
1 wineglass strong stock (made from the giblets — see page 134)
1 wineglass white wine
salt and pepper
bouquet garni (with a strip of orange rind)
1 red pepper
1 large orange
4 large green olives (cut into shreds)
1 tablespoon chopped parsley

Method

Joint the chicken. Heat a large sauté, or frying, pan and put in the oil, then the butter. When foaming, put in the joints of chicken, skin side down, and sauté until golden-brown. Turn them over and sauté on the other side. Remove the pieces from the pan, add the onion to the pan and allow to colour very slightly. Stir in the flour, add the stock and the wine and bring to the boil. Season, and replace the joints of chicken and add the bouquet garni; cover the pan and simmer on cooker top or in moderate oven, pre-set at 350°F or Mark 4, for 20-25 minutes.

Meanwhile grill the pepper, or toast in a flame, until it is charred all over, then remove the skin with a knife; cut the flesh into shreds and take out the seeds. If necessary, rinse it under the cold tap. Remove rind and the pith from the orange; slice into rounds. Shred the olives, discarding the stones.

To dish up, take up the chicken joints, trim them and arrange in a hot serving dish. Add the pepper, orange, olives and parsley to the sauce, boil up well and spoon over the dish. Serve with boiled new, potatoes or sauté potatoes (see page 139), and green beans.

*Left : removing skin from red pepper after it has been charred under grill
Right : Chicken Majorca, coated with sauce containing red pepper, orange, olives and chopped parsley*

Chicken casserole au chou

1 large roasting chicken
  (weighing 3 ½ - 4 lb)
bacon fat, or butter
about ½ pint stock (see page 134)
1 medium-size firm cabbage
  (preferably of the Dutch type)
1 onion
1 cooking, or tart dessert, apple
6-8 oz salt belly pork (cut into
  lardons)
salt and pepper
2 wineglasses dry cider
6-8 oz chipolata, or cocktail,
  sausages
chopped parsley (to garnish)

Method

Set oven at 375-400°F or Mark
5-6. Rub the bird all over with
the bacon fat (or butter) and
put a small piece inside ; set in
a roasting tin and pour round
the stock. Put to roast in the
pre-set oven for 40-45 minutes,
basting frequently and turning
the bird on its sides to get it
thoroughly brown all over.

Meanwhile shred the cabbage,
slice the onion, and peel, quarter,
core and slice the apple. Melt
1-2 tablespoons fat (or butter) in
a flameproof casserole. Put in
the onion and lardons of pork ;
cook for a few minutes, then
put in the cabbage with the
apple. Season well. Pour over
the cider and cover with a piece
of thickly buttered paper, or foil,
and the lid. Start to cook on top
of stove then put in the oven,
underneath chicken. Cook for
approximately 20 minutes. Take
out, pour off the liquid and set
aside. Joint the chicken, trim

*Adding shredded cabbage and
apple slices to onion and pork*

*Arranging the partially cooked
chicken joints on top of cabbage*

and arrange joints on top of the cabbage. Deglaze the roasting tin with the juice from the cabbage and a little extra stock (or cider). Season well and strain juices over the chicken. Cover the casserole lightly and return to the oven for a further 20-30 minutes, lowering the heat to 350°F or Mark 4.

Meanwhile fry or grill the sausages ; just before serving, surround the chicken with them, either whole or cut in half diagonally. Dust the dish well with parsley. Serve with boiled potatoes.

Chicken casserole au chou is garnished with sausages and parsley

Cuisses de poulet Xérès

5-6 whole leg joints of chicken
1 shallot
2 oz butter
2-3 tablespoons fresh white bread-
    crumbs
2-3 tablespoons chicken stock
salt and pepper
pinch of ground mace
1 large onion (sliced)
2 large carrots (sliced)
1 stick of celery (sliced)
bouquet garni
¾-1 pint jellied chicken stock (see
    page 134)

For sauce
1½ oz butter
1¼ oz plain flour
¾ pint stock (see method)
3-4 fl oz double cream

For garnish
nut of butter
2 medium-size carrots
1 glass sherry, or Madeira

1 *Boning out the leg joints : here
a drumstick is being removed*
2 *Tying up boned and stuffed
chicken joints before cooking them*

Method

Cut through the leg joints between the drumstick and thigh
and bone out the joints. Trim
the meat from the chicken
carcass and mince the trimmings together with one portion of thigh. Soften the shallot
in 1 oz of the butter and when
cold add to the minced chicken
and breadcrumbs and pound
well. Work in the 2-3 tablespoons stock, a little at a time,
and season well with the salt,
pepper and mace. Fill this mixture into the boned-out joints
and tie with thread. Set the
oven at 350° F or Mark 4.

Melt the remaining 1 oz
butter in a flameproof casserole,
add the sliced vegetables, cover
and cook slowly on top of stove
until they begin to colour. Place
prepared chicken on top, tuck
in bouquet garni and pour over
jellied stock. Season well, cover
with a buttered paper and bring
to the boil. Cover tightly and
cook in the pre-set oven for
50-60 minutes.

To make the sauce : melt the
butter, stir in the flour and cook
slowly until straw coloured. Set

aside. Take up the chicken, strain off the stock and reduce to $\frac{3}{4}$ pint. Blend this into the roux and stir until boiling. Leave to simmer until syrupy.

Cut the red part of the carrot in fine strips and put into a small pan with a nut of butter and the sherry. Cover and simmer until the carrot is tender.

Add the cream and carrots to the sauce. Remove the thread from the chicken joints, place them in a hot serving dish and spoon over the sauce. Serve with glazed carrots and plainly boiled rice (see pages 136 and 139).

Cuisses de poulet Xérès : chicken joints in cream sauce, served with glazed carrots and boiled rice

Chicken casserole italienne
with buttered noodles

3 ½ lb roasting chicken
1 oz butter
1 onion (finely chopped)
4 teaspoons tomato purée
½ pint chicken stock (made from the giblets — see page 134)
salt and pepper
bouquet garni
1 teaspoon cornflour, or arrowroot
1 can button mushrooms (7½ oz)
2 oz cooked ham (shredded)
parsley (chopped) — to garnish

Method

Brown the chicken on all sides in the butter in a flameproof casserole. Allow at least 10 minutes for this as the chicken has little or no fat between the skin and flesh and, if browned quickly, tends to become dry. Always start by browning the breast, first on one side and then the other and finish with the back or underside. In this way there is no danger of the breast getting discoloured or damaged should the butter start to over-brown, and your chicken will be the right way up for cooking.

Add the onion to the casserole and continue cooking slowly until golden-brown ; blend in the tomato purée and stock, season, add the bouquet garni and bring to the boil. Cover the casserole tightly and continue cooking slowly on top of the stove or in the oven, pre-set at 350°F or Mark 4, until the bird is tender — about 50-60 minutes. Take out the chicken and keep hot while you thicken the sauce in the casserole with the corn-flour, or arrowroot, mixed to a paste with 1 tablespoon stock or water, and boil up well. Add the mushrooms and ham.

Carve the chicken into neat joints and put back in the casserole. Finish with chopped parsley and serve the buttered noodles separately.

Buttered noodles

Allow 6 oz noodles for 4 people
1 oz butter
salt
black pepper (ground from mill)

Method

Cook in plenty of boiling salted water, at least 2 quarts. Do not break but put one end of the noodles into the fast boiling water ; as ends soften, coil round the pan. Reboil, then lower the heat so that the water just simmers. Stir gently from time to time to prevent noodles sticking together or to the bottom of the pan. When cooked (about 20 minutes) they should look creamy and opaque — a good test is when they can be just severed with the thumbnail.
Watchpoint Do not overcook noodles because they become sticky and floury.

Strain at once into a colander, pour over a large jug of hot water to rinse off starch and drain well. Rinse the used pan, add a large knob of butter, put back the noodles and toss over

the heat for 2-3 minutes, and season. If the noodles have to be kept hot before serving, pour about $\frac{1}{2}$ pint of hand-hot water into the rinsed cooking pan, put in the noodles, cover and keep on one side. When ready to serve, strain off and toss in butter as described.

Buttered noodles are good served with chicken casserole italienne, and make a change from potatoes

Chicken bonne femme

3 lb chicken
1 oz butter
3 oz streaky bacon (in the piece)
2 oz mushrooms
12 button onions, or spring onions
1 tablespoon plain flour
$\frac{3}{4}$-1 pint stock (see page 134)
bouquet garni
2-3 medium-size potatoes, or 8-10
 baby new potatoes
parsley (chopped) — to garnish

Bonne femme is the name given to dishes incorporating the classic garnish of onions, bacon and mushrooms.

Method

Heat a large casserole, drop in the butter and, when foaming, put in the chicken, breast-side downwards. Brown the bird slowly on all sides. Allow at least 10 minutes for this as the chicken has little or no fat between the skin and flesh and, if browned quickly, tends to become dry. Always start by browning the breast first on one side and then the other and finish with the back or underside. In this way there is no danger of the breast getting discoloured or damaged should the butter start to overbrown.

Set oven at 350°F or Mark 4.

Meanwhile, de-rind the bacon piece and cut it into short strips. Quarter mushrooms. Blanch the whole onions with the bacon in a pan of cold water (bring to the boil and drain well). Take chicken out of casserole, add onions, bacon and mushrooms and allow to colour. Now joint the chicken.

Add the flour to the casserole, pour on the stock and bring to the boil. Replace the chicken joints and add the bouquet garni, cover casserole and cook for up to 1 hour in the pre-set oven. After 20 minutes, add the potatoes (cut lengthways into four, and trim off the sharp edge with a potato peeler) ; leave new potatoes whole. When potatoes are tender, remove bouquet garni, serve sprinkled with plenty of chopped parsley.

Watchpoint Ready-jointed pieces of chicken may be used, but joints must be trimmed of rough bone ; brown them on the skin side only as the less tender underside can become hard when browned.

Game dishes

Game is a term that covers wild birds and animals that are protected by law and may be shot and sold only within certain periods or seasons of the year. Only people possessing a game licence (usually poulterers and fishmongers) are allowed to sell game over the counter. Although rabbits and pigeons are not classed as game, for they may be shot at any time of the year, for convenience they are sold on the same counter and are often prepared like game.

The seasons when game used in our recipes is available are given below — these dates do vary a little from time to time as the animals' breeding habits vary, and the ones we give are the latest available for Great Britain. Rabbits are at their best from September to February, and pigeons from March to October.

All game needs hanging if the flesh is to be tender and well-flavoured. The length of hanging time allowed depends on personal taste and the weather ; warm, damp conditions will cause the flesh to decompose more rapidly than in cold weather. Do not pluck or draw game before hanging. Game birds are ready when the tail feathers are easy to pull.

Ideally, any game you buy should have been shot in the head, leaving the body unmarked. Badly shot game should be hung for a shorter time and needs careful watching to see that it does not go 'off'.

Game seasons
Venison : late June to January
Grouse : 12 August —
10 December
Hare : August to February
Pheasant : 1 October —
1 February
Partridge : 1 September —
1 February

Game casserole

2 lb venison, or moose (a piece cut from the shoulder blade, saddle, or haunch of venison)
1 teaspoon salt
¼ teaspoon pepper (ground from mill)
1 bayleaf (crushed or cut in small pieces)
½ teaspoon rosemary
½-¾ pint milk
½ lb pickled belly pork
1 oz plain flour
1 teaspoon paprika pepper
about 1 tablespoon salad oil
1 oz butter
2 large onions (finely sliced)
1 pint jellied stock (see page 134)
2 wineglasses red wine
1 small carton (2½ fl oz) soured cream
juice of ½ small lemon

Method

If using moose cut away any fat. Cut the moose or venison into 1-inch cubes, place in a casserole or bowl, sprinkle with the seasonings and herbs and pour over the milk. Cover and leave in the refrigerator for 24 hours, turning occasionally.

Cover the pork with cold water and bring to the boil, drain and cut into dice. Drain the milk off the meat, mix the flour and paprika together and dust enough over the meat to coat each piece and to dry the surface.

Heat the salad oil in a flame-proof casserole, add the pork and cook until the dice are golden-brown on all sides. Add the butter to the casserole and, when foaming, put in the meat a few pieces at a time and cook fairly quickly until pieces are lightly coloured. Remove meat from the fat with a draining spoon. When all the meat has been browned in this way and removed from the casserole, add the onions, lower the heat and cook slowly, stirring from time to time, until golden-brown.

Add the stock and wine and bring to the boil. Return the meat to the casserole, cover and simmer very gently for about 2 hours or until tender. This could be done on top of the stove or in the oven, set at 325°F or Mark 3.

Mix any remaining flour and paprika with the soured cream and lemon juice and add to the casserole. Stir until mixture thickens and taste for seasoning. Serve with creamed potatoes (see page 30).

Pigeons in tomato sauce

4 pigeons
1 oz butter
1 large onion (sliced)
1 dessertspoon plain flour
4 oz mushrooms, or small can of mushrooms
$\frac{3}{4}$ pint tomato sauce (see method)

Method

Split pigeons in two, first cutting down to breastbone with a knife, then through bone and carcass with scissors. Trim away carcass bone. Slowly brown halves on skin side only in hot butter in a frying pan. Then take out halves and pack into a casserole. Set the oven at 350°F or Mark 4.

Cook the sliced onion for 4-5 minutes in the pan, adding a little extra butter, if necessary. Take out onion and lay on top of pigeon halves in casserole.

If using fresh mushrooms, sauté briskly in pan of hot butter and set aside.

To prepare a quick tomato sauce ; use a small can of Italian tomato sauce (not purée), make it up to $\frac{3}{4}$ pint with stock and thicken with kneaded butter or with a roux made with 1 dessertspoon flour and $\frac{3}{4}$ oz butter. Add to mushrooms. (If using canned mushrooms, add them now.)

Pour tomato sauce over pigeons, cover casserole tightly and cook for 1-1$\frac{1}{2}$ hours, or until pigeons are tender, in the preset oven.

Pigeons casseroled in tomato sauce

Pigeons with raisins

4 pigeons
4-6 oz streaky bacon rashers
1½ oz butter
½-¾ pint brown jellied stock (see page 134)
16 button onions
2-3 oz raisins (stoned)

Method

Split pigeons in two and trim away the carcass bone with scissors. Set the oven at 325°F or Mark 3.

Cut rashers into short strips, blanch (put in cold water, bring to the boil). Fry in the butter in a pan for 2-3 minutes, then take out and put in the pigeons. Brown slowly on skin side only. Take out halves and pack into a casserole with the bacon ; season and pour over the stock barely to cover. Bring to boil, cover tightly and cook for 1-1½ hours in the pre-set oven.

Meanwhile peel onions and brown in the pan, giving them a dusting of caster sugar. Add to casserole after first 30 minutes.

Have raisins ready soaked in hot water to plump them up. Drain and add to casserole 15 minutes before serving. At end of cooking time the gravy should be well reduced (brown and sticky). This is why jellied stock is essential, otherwise gravy will need thickening with kneaded butter or arrowroot.

Pigeons Saint-Germain

4 pigeons
2 oz slice of salt belly pork, or green streaky bacon
12 pickling-size onions (blanched)
1 tablespoon plain flour
7½ fl oz chicken stock (see page 134), or canned consommé
2 lb fresh green peas (shelled)
3 juniper berries, or pinch of ground allspice (Jamaica pepper)
sprig of thyme
salt and pepper
7½ fl oz apple juice
kneaded butter, or slaked arrowroot (optional)

Method

Cut the pork or bacon into dice, put in a heavy flameproof casserole and place over gentle heat to draw out the fat. Add the pigeons and onions to the pan ; cook until brown on all sides, then remove from the pan. Blend in the flour, cook until russet-brown, pour in stock and stir until smooth.

Replace the pigeons and onions, add the shelled green peas, juniper berries, thyme and seasoning. Cover and simmer gently on top of stove for about 40 minutes.

To serve : take up the pigeons, split in half and cut away the backbone and legs (these can be used to make a good game soup). Return the pigeon breasts to the casserole, pour on the apple juice and reheat. Taste for seasoning. The sauce should be the consistency of cream. Add extra thickening, if necessary ; either kneaded butter or slaked arrowroot.

Stuffed pigeons St. Cyr

4 pigeons
1½ oz butter
1 wineglass white wine
¼ pint strong veal stock (see page 134)
salt and pepper

For stuffing
2 oz mushrooms
2 oz butter
½ lemon
6 oz raw minced veal, or lean pork
2 oz tongue (chopped)

For garnish
2 lb green peas
1 lettuce heart (washed and quartered)
2 oz butter
salt and pepper
2 teaspoons granulated sugar
4 tablespoons water
½ lb small new carrots
12 small button onions
4 slices of cooked tongue

Below : cutting rib cage away from pigeon. Right : placing vegetable garnish in the centre of the dish

Method

Set oven at 350°F or Mark 4. Cut the pigeons down the back, remove back and carcass bone.

To prepare the stuffing : trim and wash the mushrooms, chop finely and put in a pan with 2 oz butter and a good squeeze of lemon ; cover and cook for 5 minutes. Then allow to cool. Mix the minced veal (or pork), tongue and cooked mushrooms together and season well. Fill the pigeons, sew and truss neatly.

Melt the 1½ oz butter in a deep cocotte, or flameproof casserole, and brown the birds slowly on all sides, season lightly, cover the pan tightly and put in pre-set moderate oven for about 1¼ hours.

Meanwhile prepare the garnish. Shell the peas and place in a flameproof casserole with the quartered lettuce heart, 1 oz of the butter, salt and pepper, 1 teaspoon sugar and 4 tablespoons water. Cover and cook gently for 15 minutes. Cut and trim the carrots into small 'barrels', cover with water, add 1 oz butter, 1 teaspoon sugar and a little salt. Cook until all the water has evaporated, then shake the pan gently, turning the

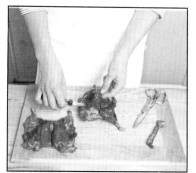

carrots until they begin to colour in the butter and sugar glaze.

Cover the onions with cold water and boil for 5 minutes, drain, add to the pan with the peas and lettuce and continue cooking for 10 minutes. Cut the cooked tongue slices in half, place them on a plate and heat over the pan of peas.

To serve : take up the pigeons, remove the string, cut in half and press the stuffing in well ; arrange in a circle on a round dish with a slice of tongue between each pigeon half. Place the peas and onions in the centre and pile the carrots on top ; keep warm. Deglaze the cocotte with the white wine, stir briskly over the heat for 1 minute then add the veal stock ; season and spoon sauce over the pigeon.

Finished dish of stuffed pigeons St. Cyr with the birds placed on slices of tongue and vegetable garnish arranged in the centre

Jugged pigeons

3 squabs, or 4 plump wood pigeons
2 onions (sliced)
½ pint brown ale, or cider
bouquet garni
½ pint good stock (see page 134)
kneaded butter
squeeze of lemon
parsley (to garnish)

For stuffing
2 hard-boiled eggs
1 cup fresh white breadcrumbs
2 tablespoons shredded suet
pigeon livers
good pinch of ground mace
2 tablespoons chopped mixed
   herbs and parsley
1 small egg (beaten)
salt and pepper

Method

Set oven at 325-350°F or Mark 3-4. First prepare stuffing : push the yolks of the hard-boiled eggs through a strainer and add to the crumbs with the suet. Reserve the whites. Blanch and chop livers and add to yolk mixture with the mace, herbs and sufficient beaten egg to moisten ; add the seasoning.

Wipe the pigeons and stuff them with the mixture. Truss them and pack into a thick flameproof casserole with the onions. Pour over the ale (or cider), add the bouquet garni and half the stock. Bring to the boil, then put in pre-set slow to moderate oven for 1-2½ hours (1 hour for squabs, longer for wood pigeons or until very tender.

Tip off the gravy into another pan and remove bouquet garni. Thicken the gravy with the kneaded butter and add rest of stock if necessary (there should be about ½-¾ pint of gravy in all). Add a squeeze of lemon and bring to the boil. If using squabs, take up and cut in half, first removing string. Leave the wood pigeons whole but remove string. Pour over the gravy and serve in the casserole.

Shred the reserved egg white, scatter it over the top and sprinkle with parsley.

Pigeons and squabs
Both wild and domesticated pigeons may be eaten. They are trussed in the same way as chickens except that the feet are left on — they are scalded and scraped and folded across the rear of the bird — and the wings are not drawn across the back. Squabs are very young pigeons, 4-6 weeks old. They are also specially bred for the table on squab farms and, being a pure breed, these are plumper and larger than the ordinary wood pigeon.
Watchpoint Cooking time in all pigeon recipes does depend on the age and size of the birds.

Pigeons en cocotte

4 pigeons
1 oz butter
4 oz green streaky bacon
12 small button onions
pinch of granulated sugar
4 oz button mushrooms
$\frac{3}{4}$ oz plain flour
1 wineglass white wine
$7\frac{1}{2}$ fl oz chicken, or veal, stock
  (see page 134)
salt and pepper

Method

Set oven at 325°F or Mark 3. Heat the butter in a flameproof casserole, put in the pigeons and brown slowly on all sides.

Remove rind from the bacon, cut into lardons and cover with cold water. Bring to the boil and simmer for 3 minutes ; drain and dry on absorbent paper. Blanch onions ; drain and dry in the same way. Remove pigeons from the casserole, add bacon and onions and cook until brown.

Watchpoint Remove bacon with a draining spoon when brown and shake pan to turn the onions without touching them, so that they remain whole. Add small pinch of sugar to help them brown.

Remove onions from casserole with a draining spoon. Wash and trim mushrooms, cut them in half and add to the casserole ; cook briskly until brown, then take out. Stir in the flour, cook until golden-brown and add the wine and stock, blend until smooth and bring to the boil. Season, then strain the sauce into a basin. Rinse and wipe out the casserole and put back the pigeons, bacon, onions and mushrooms. Then pour over the sauce and bring to the boil ; cover tightly and put in pre-set oven for 2 hours.

Pigeons en cocotte normande

4 pigeons
1 oz dripping, or butter
1 medium-size onion (sliced)
3 medium-size cooking apples
$\frac{3}{4}$ oz plain flour
$\frac{1}{2}$ pint stock (see page 134)
$\frac{1}{4}$ pint cider
salt and pepper
bouquet garni
4 rashers of streaky bacon
1 tablespoon chopped parsley
  (to garnish)

Method

Set oven at 350°F or Mark 4.

Brown the pigeons slowly in the dripping (or butter) in a flameproof casserole, then remove them from the pan, cut in half and trim away backbone.

Add the onion to the pan and allow it to colour. Wipe and core one of the apples, cut it in slices and put in the pan with the onion ; increase the heat and continue cooking until brown. Dust in the flour, cook for a further 2 minutes and then pour on the stock and cider. Bring to the boil, season, add bouquet garni and the pigeons. Cover the casserole tightly and cook in pre-set oven for $1\frac{1}{2}$ hours.

Take up the pigeons and arrange them in an entrée dish. Strain the sauce, reduce it over quick heat if too thin, and then spoon it over the pigeons. Cut the remaining apples in thick slices (about $\frac{1}{2}$ inch), and stamp out the cores with a small pastry cutter. Fry the bacon rashers until brown and crisp and place them on top of the pigeon. Fry the apple rings in the bacon fat very quickly until brown. Arrange the apple rings round the pigeons and dust with the parsley.

Casseroled rabbit with mustard

1-2 rabbits (jointed)
dash of vinegar
salt
$\frac{1}{4}$-$\frac{1}{2}$ lb streaky bacon, or pickled
    pork (in the piece)
2 tablespoons bacon fat, or
    dripping
4 medium-size onions (quartered)
1 tablespoon plain flour
1 pint stock (see page 134)
pepper (ground from mill)
bouquet garni
1 small carton double cream, or
    evaporated milk
1 dessertspoon French mustard
1 dessertspoon chopped parsley

Wild rabbit is intended for this dish but, if you prefer, Ostend (tame) rabbit or a cut of shoulder of veal can be substituted.

Method

Trim the pieces of rabbit into neat joints, cutting the wings (forelegs) in two and trimming off the rib-cage. Soak the joints overnight in plenty of salted water with a dash of vinegar to remove the strong rabbit flavour. Then drain joints, rinse and dry thoroughly.

Cut away rind and rust (brown rim on underside) from bacon, or the skin from the pork. Cut into large dice and blanch by putting into cold water, bringing to boil and simmering for 15-20 minutes. Then drain. Set oven at 350°F or Mark 4.

Heat dripping in a thick flameproof casserole and lightly brown rabbit joints in it. Take out rabbit and put in bacon and quartered onions ; fry well until coloured, draw aside, stir in flour and pour on stock. Bring to boil, grind in a little pepper, add bouquet garni and rabbit joints. Cover casserole and cook for $1\frac{1}{2}$ hours, or until rabbit is really tender, in pre-set oven.

Draw aside, take out bouquet garni and add the cream mixed with mustard and chopped parsley. Adjust seasoning and reheat before serving.

Lentil purée

6 oz Egyptian lentils
1 onion (stuck with clove)
1 carrot (cut in rounds)
salt and pepper
bouquet garni
stock (optional)
2 oz butter
celery (chopped)

This is an excellent accompaniment to casseroled rabbit. Dried peas can be used instead of the Egyptian lentils.

Method

Soak lentils overnight, drain, cook in plenty of water brought slowly to boil, with onion, carrot (cut into thick rounds), bouquet garni and a little salt. Simmer until tender.

Sieve lentil mixture, lighten with stock if it is too thick, draw aside from heat and beat in butter with a little pepper.

Before serving, stir into purée a little raw, chopped celery.

Rabbit and bacon casserole

1 rabbit
dash of vinegar
2 tablespoons dripping
1 small onion (finely chopped)
1 tablespoon plain flour
¾-1 pint stock (see page 134)
bouquet garni
1 rounded teaspoon tomato purée
1 clove of garlic (chopped)
salt and pepper
4 oz streaky bacon (in the piece)
12 pickling onions, or shallots

Method

Joint rabbit, trim and soak overnight in salted water with a dash of vinegar. Drain and dry well.

Set oven at 350°F or Mark 4.

Brown joints slowly in hot dripping in a thick flameproof casserole. Add chopped onion, sprinkle in flour. Turn joints over to coat them in mixture and fry for 1 minute. Then draw aside, add enough stock barely to cover, add bouquet garni, tomato purée and garlic. Season lightly, cover pan tightly and cook for 30 minutes in the pre-set oven. Meanwhile, cut bacon into short strips, blanch with pickling onions or shallots (put in cold water, bring to boil). Then drain and add to rabbit. Continue to cook for 1 hour or until all is tender. Remove bouquet garni, serve in casserole.

Rabbit paysanne

2 young rabbits (jointed)
2 oz plain flour (seasoned with salt, pepper and curry powder)
6 oz fat salt belly pork
2 large onions (thinly sliced)
6-8 oz streaky bacon rashers (No. 4 cut)
½ pint stock (see page 134), or ¼ dry cider and ¼ pint stock
2 tablespoons chopped parsley

Method

Trim rabbit joints and soak overnight in salted water.

Rinse and dry the joints thoroughly. Roll the joints in the seasoned flour, keeping at least 1 tablespoon in reserve to use as thickening. Cut pork into dice and put in a deep frying pan ; set on gentle heat to allow the fat to run. Then add onion, increase heat and fry gently until just coloured ; remove pork and onion from pan with a slice.

Wrap each rabbit joint in a whole rasher, or half, of bacon ; put into the pan and allow to brown slowly.

Watchpoint If the fat is insufficient when frying the rabbit joints, add a little dripping or lard.

Take rabbit out, put back pork and onions and set rabbit joints on top. Pour in a good ¼ pint stock (or cider), cover and simmer until tender (about 45 minutes). Then mix reserved flour (about 1 tablespoon) with about ¼ pint stock. Draw aside the pan and when off the boil pour in the stock and flour mixture, add parsley ; shake gently and reboil. Serve hot.

Braised rabbit with tomatoes

1-2 young rabbits (depending on size)
seasoned flour
4 oz salt belly pork (or thick slice of green streaky bacon)
$2\frac{1}{2}$ fl oz oil
15 small pickling onions
scant $\frac{1}{2}$ pint jellied stock (see page 134)
salt and pepper
2 tablespoons single cream
6 small tomatoes
pinch of caster sugar

Method
Soak the jointed rabbit in salted water overnight.

Set oven at 350°F or Mark 4. Dry joints thoroughly, then roll them in seasoned flour. Cut the pork into lardons (thick strips). Heat a cocotte, or flame-proof casserole, with two-thirds of the oil and add the lardons of pork. Add the rabbit and colour lightly on all sides. Then brown the onions and add the stock ; season and put in the pre-set oven to cook for 50-60 minutes, longer for an older rabbit. Baste from time to time and allow the stock to reduce almost to a glaze during cooking. When done, add the cream.

Scald and skin the tomatoes and cut them in half. Scoop

out the seeds. Heat the remaining oil in a frying pan and when hot put in the tomatoes, cut side down ; when coloured, turn, season, add the sugar and cook until just brown.

Take up the rabbit. Test for seasoning and pour sauce over the rabbit. Garnish with the tomatoes.

Colouring floured rabbit joints in oil with lardons of salt belly pork

Arranging finished dish of the braised rabbit joints with tomatoes

Casserole of grouse

2 grouse
1 oz butter, or dripping
1 carrot
1 small turnip
2 onions
2-3 sticks of celery
$\frac{1}{2}$-$\frac{3}{4}$ pint stock (see page 134)
bouquet garni
1 wineglass red wine
salt and pepper
glazed onions (to garnish)

Method

Melt butter in a thick flameproof casserole, wipe grouse, brown slowly in butter. Remove grouse from casserole and keep hot.

Dice vegetables and sweat, ie. cook slowly until all fat is absorbed, then allow to colour slightly. Add stock, bring to boil, add bouquet garni, grouse and red wine, flamed. To flame wine, heat it gently in a small pan and set it alight. When flame burns out, alcohol will have evaporated. Season, cover pan tightly and cook slowly on top of stove for 40 minutes. Baste regularly with gravy.

Dish up grouse, remove bouquet garni, garnish with glazed onions (see page 137).

Marinated, jugged grouse

2 good, old grouse
scant $\frac{1}{2}$ pint stock (see page 134)
$\frac{3}{4}$ lb chuck steak
a little dripping
1 medium-size onion (finely chopped)
bouquet garni
1-1$\frac{1}{2}$ wineglasses port, or red wine
1 tablespoon redcurrant jelly (see page 139)
pinch of ground mace
forcement balls (see page 137)

Method
Split the grouse, trim away the backbones and add the bones to the measured stock. Put into a pan, cover and simmer for 20-30 minutes and then strain.

Set oven at 325°F or Mark 3.

Cut the steak into $\frac{1}{2}$-inch pieces and brown quickly in a little hot dripping. Take out of the pan, add the grouse and the onion, lower the heat and allow just to colour. Then layer the steak and grouse together in a casserole and season well. Tuck in the bouquet garni and pour over the prepared stock. Add the wine, redcurrant jelly and mace, cover tightly and cook in the pre-set oven.

Prepare forcemeat balls and set aside. After 1 hour's cooking, remove the casserole lid and place the forcement balls on top. Cover again and continue to cook for a further hour, when the meat should be very tender. If wished, 10-15 minutes before the dish is ready, remove the lid and allow the forcemeat balls to brown. Pour in a little more port just before serving. Serve with braised red cabbage (see page 131) and creamed potatoes (see page 30).

Fricassée of hare with chestnuts

1 good-size hare (with blood)
few drops of vinegar
2-3 tablespoons olive oil
1$\frac{1}{2}$-2 fl oz brandy
1 small onion (sliced)
pepper (ground from mill)
$\frac{1}{2}$ lb pickled pork
1 oz butter
1 tablespoon plain flour
$\frac{1}{2}$ bottle red wine
salt and pepper
bouquet garni with stick of celery
1 clove of garlic (crushed)
$\frac{1}{2}$ lb button onions (blanched)
$\frac{1}{2}$-$\frac{3}{4}$ lb chestnuts
$\frac{1}{2}$-$\frac{3}{4}$ pint good stock (see page 134)

Method
Cut up the hare in small neat pieces (or have this done for you). Reserve the blood and add a few drops of vinegar to it to prevent it coagulating. Put the hare into a dish and sprinkle with the olive oil, brandy and onion. Grind over a little pepper, cover and leave to marinate for some hours, or overnight, either in a cool place or in the refrigerator.

Simmer the pork in water to cover for 30-40 minutes, cool slightly in the liquid, then take up and cut into cubes. Take the hare from the marinade and dab the pieces dry with absorbent paper. Brown the pieces lightly in a flameproof casserole, using about 1 oz butter. Add the pork and, after a few minutes, stir in the flour. Pour on the wine, which should just cover the hare, season lightly and add the bouquet garni and the garlic. Bring to the boil, then cover and simmer very slowly on top of the stove, or put the casserole in the oven (pre-set at 325°F or Mark 3) for 2$\frac{1}{2}$-3 hours. After 1 hour add the button onions and continue to cook until the hare and the onions are tender. Meanwhile scald and skin the chestnuts (see page 85), then simmer in good stock barely to cover for 35-40 minutes until tender.

At the end of the cooking time remove the bouquet garni and taste for seasoning. Add the reserved blood to the gravy in the pan as if it were a liaison. Bring to boiling point, but do not actually boil.

Dish up the hare and garnish with the chestnuts. Serve very hot.

Note : the hare will cook well in an enamelled iron casserole and the chestnuts can be added to it for serving. Should the liquid reduce rather too much, add a little additional stock, but this is best avoided.

Serve with creamed potatoes (see page 30) and baby brussels sprouts.

Fricassée of hare with chestnuts can be served straight from the casserole in which it is cooked

Hare in beer

1 hare (jointed)
½ pint brown ale
1 clove of garlic (crushed with salt)
1 bayleaf
4 large onions (finely sliced)
¼ teaspoon grated nutmeg
1 tablespoon plain flour
1 teaspoon paprika pepper
1 tablespoon beef dripping
½ pint stock (see page 134)
1 teaspoon red wine vinegar
1 carrot (grated)
6 potatoes
little extra dripping, or butter

Method

Wipe the hare joints, put them in a large mixing bowl and cover with the beer, garlic, bayleaf, sliced onions and nutmeg. Mix together, cover and leave to marinate in the refrigerator for 24 hours.

Set oven at 350°F or Mark 4. Remove the pieces of hare from the marinade and wipe dry on absorbent paper ; roll them in the flour mixed with the paprika. Heat the dripping in a flameproof casserole, put in the joints of hare and brown slowly over a moderate heat. Blend in the stock and vinegar and add the marinade, including the onions and herbs. Add the grated carrot and bring to the boil. Cover pan and put in pre-set oven for about 1¼ hours.

Boil the potatoes, cut in ¼-inch slices and arrange them on the top of the hare. Baste them with a little of the stock in the pan, dot with a few pieces of dripping or butter and return to the oven and continue cooking uncovered for a further 30-40 minutes or until the potatoes are quite soft.

Marinated hare

1 hare
marinade (as previous recipe)
1-2 tablespoons French mustard
1-2 oz butter
salt and pepper
2½ oz jellied stock (see page 134)
kneaded butter (made from fat
    skimmed from the gravy and
    1 dessertspoon plain flour)
2½ fl oz double cream

Method

Wipe the hare and joint it, cutting away the rib cage and the wings. Put the joints in a deep dish and pour over the marinade ; leave for 24 hours or longer, turning and basting occasionally.

Take out pieces of hare, wipe them dry and spread with the French mustard. Heat a thick enamelled iron cocotte, or casserole, drop in the butter, put into it the joints of hare and sauté rather gently until just turning colour. Add the strained marinade, a little seasoning and the stock. Cover and cook gently on top of cooker, or in the oven, pre-set at 350°F or Mark 4, for about 35-40 minutes or until the hare is very tender.

Take hare out and dish up ; boil up the liquid well, draw aside and thicken slightly with a little kneaded butter. Add the cream, boil up, adjust seasoning and spoon sauce over the hare. Serve with creamed potato (see page 30).

Jugged hare (Civet de lièvre)

1 good hare (with the blood)
1½ oz butter
4 oz rasher of streaky bacon (cut into lardons and blanched)
24 pickling onions (blanched)
1 oz plain flour
1 pint red wine
1 pint stock
4 oz button mushrooms

For marinade
4 tablespoons olive oil
2-3 tablespoons brandy
1 large onion (cut into rings)
3 shallots
3 sprigs of parsley (with the root on if possible)
½ bayleaf
sprig of thyme

To garnish
triangular croûtes of fried bread

Method

Cut the hare, detaching the legs and dividing the back into 3 or 4 pieces, and put the pieces in the marinade. Leave in a cool place for 24 hours, turning the hare from time to time. Reserve the blood.

Heat the butter in a large flameproof casserole and brown the lardons of bacon. Remove bacon from the pan and place on a plate. Add pickling onions to the pan; cook slowly until well coloured and then add to the lardons and set on one side.

Add the flour to the fat in the pan and cook slowly until golden-brown. Meanwhile, remove the pieces of hare from the marinade and add them to the pan; cook with the roux until nicely coloured on all sides (about 10 minutes). Add the wine and stock, stir well and bring to the boil. Cover with a round of buttered paper and a tightly fitting lid; put in a very moderate oven, pre-set at 325°F or Mark 3, for about 1½ hours.

Take up the hare and strain the sauce; wipe out the casserole, replace the hare and add the mushrooms and prepared bacon and onions. Pour the strained sauce over the hare and return casserole to the oven for 15-20 minutes.

Just before serving, thicken the sauce with the blood and surround with the croûtes.

Pheasant vallée d'Auge

1 large pheasant, or 2 hen
   pheasants
1½ oz butter
2 medium-size apples (cooking
   or dessert apples)
1 medium-size onion (finely
   sliced)
2-3 sticks celery (sliced)
1 tablespoon plain flour
1¼ wineglasses white wine
½-¾ pint jellied stock (see page 134)
salt and pepper
1 small carton (2½ fl oz) double
   cream
chopped parsley

For garnish
1 head of celery
1 green pepper, or pimiento (cut
   into rings) — optional
2 Cox's apples
1 oz butter
caster sugar

Dusting apple rings with sugar for garnish to pheasant vallée d'Auge

Garnishing dish with celery bundles, apple rings and château potatoes

This is one of the best of pheasant dishes and is especially suitable for a party, in which case use 2 hen pheasants.

Method

Brown the birds slowly and carefully all over in the butter in a flameproof casserole. Meanwhile quarter, core and slice the apples. When the birds are browned take them out of the casserole and put in the onion, celery, and apples ; sauté gently for 5-6 minutes. Stir in the flour, off the heat, and add the wine and stock. Bring to the boil, season and turn out into a bowl. Put pheasants back in casserole and pour over sauce ; cover with greaseproof paper or foil and the lid and simmer on top of the stove or cook in a moderate oven, pre-set at 350°F or Mark 4, for 45-50 minutes.

Meanwhile prepare garnish. Separate celery into sticks, cut these into 2-2½ inch strips. Tie in bundles, using a 4-5 inch length of string for each one for lifting out of saucepan. Cook for about 12 minutes in boiling salted water. Remove the string and put a ring of pepper around each bundle.

Wipe the second lot of apples, cut crossways in ¼-½ inch thick slices and stamp out the core with an apple corer. Fry slices quickly in butter and dust well with caster sugar. Do this on full heat and allow about 1½-2 minutes on each side. When browned, lift carefully on to a greased plate and keep hot.

Watchpoint If apple rings are overcooked, they become wrinkled and do not look very appetising when served.

When the birds are tender take them out of the casserole and strain the sauce, pushing as much of the vegetable and apple mixture through the strainer as possible. Turn into a saucepan, adjust the seasoning and boil up well. When a syrupy consistency, add the cream, whisking it well in. Leave to simmer while the birds are carved. Dish them up and spoon over enough of the sauce to coat nicely ; serve the rest separately. Garnish dish with celery bundles and apple rings. Dust with parsley, and serve château potatoes (see page 138).

Pheasant en cocotte

1 good-size cock pheasant
pepper (ground from mill)
ground allspice (optional)
1-2 oz butter
1-2 glasses brown sherry
1 small can (8 oz) Italian tomatoes

For stuffing
1 small onion (finely chopped)
1 scant oz butter
4 oz veal (minced)
2 oz fresh white breadcrumbs
3-4 oz chicken livers
good pinch of dried thyme, or
    marjoram
salt and pepper

trussing needle and fine string

Below : for pheasant en cocotte, the boned out bird is filled with stuffing Right : the stuffed pheasant is then sewn up before being reshaped and trussed for cooking in casserole

Method

Make sure the skin of the pheasant is not broken. Then slit it down the back and bone out the carcass, thigh bones and breast bone. Leave in the wing pinions and drum sticks. When boned, lay bird flat on the board cut side uppermost and grind over pepper, and sprinkle on a little allspice if liked.

To prepare the stuffing, soften the onion in the butter, turn into a basin and add the minced veal and breadcrumbs. Slice the chicken livers finely, using a scraping movement of the knife and removing any strings, etc. Add these to the bowl of stuffing with the herbs and seasoning. Mix the stuffing, then fill the pheasant with it, sew up, reshape and truss.

Heat an iron cocotte or thick flameproof casserole, drop in a good oz of the butter and put

in the bird, breast side downwards. Cook it slowly until brown on all sides. Heat 1 glass of sherry, allow it to catch alight, then pour it blazing over the bird. Cook for 1-2 minutes until there is a sticky brown glaze on the bottom of the pan. Slightly mash the tomatoes with a fork and pour them round the pheasant. Season ; cover with a piece of greaseproof paper and the lid. Cook slowly on top of the stove or in a moderate oven (pre-set at 350°F or Mark 4) for about 40-45 minutes.

Then take up the pheasant, remove the string and dish up. Rub the contents of the pan through a strainer and add, if wished, a second glass of sherry. Turn this sauce into a small pan, boil up and pour over and around the pheasant. Serve with château potatoes and braised celery (see pages 138 and 77).

Stuffed pheasant alsacienne

1 plump pheasant
1½-2 oz butter (for roasting)
1 glass sherry
1 wineglass stock (see page 134)
bouquet garni
2-3 sticks of celery

For farce
1 medium-size onion (finely chopped)
good ½ oz butter
6 oz pork (minced)
2 tablespoons fresh white breadcrumbs
1 teaspoon chopped sage
salt and pepper
1 egg yolk

For sauce
2-3 cooking apples
½ oz butter
salt and pepper
granulated sugar (to taste)
2-3 tablespoons cider
1 tablespoon arrowroot (slaked with 2 tablespoons water)
2½ fl oz double cream

Trussing needle and fine string

This is served with an apple sauce flavoured with cider and with cream added. Also served separately are süsskraut, and château potatoes (see page 138).

Method
Bone out the pheasant, leaving in the leg bones.

To prepare the farce ; soften the onion in the butter. Add this to the pork with the breadcrumbs and sage. Season and bind with the egg yolk. Fill the pheasant with this stuffing, re-shape, sew up and truss. Brown carefully in hot butter in a flame-proof casserole, then flame with the sherry. Add stock, bouquet garni and sliced celery.

Cover tightly and simmer on low heat or in the oven, pre-set at 350°F or Mark 4, for 45-50 minutes.

Meanwhile prepare the sauce. Slice the apples without peeling them and cook to a pulp with the butter. Rub through a strainer and return to the pan. Season and add sugar to taste, then pour on the cider. Simmer for 5 minutes.

Take up, carve and dish up the pheasant. Strain the gravy, add to the sauce with the cream and thicken it slightly with a little slaked arrowroot. Spoon some over pheasant ; serve rest separately.

Süsskraut

1 small Dutch cabbage
1-2 oz butter
2 tablespoons wine vinegar
1 tablespoon caster sugar
salt and pepper
1 tablespoon chopped parsley

Method
Wash and shred cabbage finely. Well rub a thick pan with butter and pack in the cabbage, adding the vinegar, sugar and seasoning. Cover with buttered paper and the pan lid and cook slowly for 20-25 minutes until the cabbage is just tender. Fork in chopped parsley just before serving.

Venison ardennaise

2½-3 lb haunch, or saddle, of
  venison
pork fat, or larding bacon
1 tablespoon dripping
1 lb large onions (finely sliced)
½ pint brown ale
¼ pint stock (see page 134)
1 clove of garlic (crushed with salt)
1 teaspoon red wine vinegar
1 teaspoon granulated sugar
bouquet garni
pepper (ground from mill)
1 dessertspoon French mustard
1 tablespoon double cream
1 tablespoon plain flour
1 can (8 oz) chestnut purée
salt
½ oz butter

For croquettes of celeriac
1 head of celeriac
seasoned flour
beaten egg
dried white breadcrumbs (see page
  136)
butter (for frying)

Method

Set the oven at 350°F or Mark
4. Lard the venison on one side
only. Heat the dripping in a
heavy flameproof casserole and
brown the onions slowly. When
they are really well coloured set
the venison on the top, pour over
the ale and stock and add the
garlic, vinegar, sugar and
bouquet garni. Season well with
black pepper, cover the pan
and cook in the pre-set oven for
1-1¼ hours. Remove the lid of the
pan, baste the meat, continue
cooking for about 15 minutes
uncovered, then remove meat
from the pan and set on a
baking sheet.

Mix the mustard and cream
together, spread over the
venison and return to the oven
until the lardons are crisp.
Meanwhile skim all the fat from
the gravy in the pan and mix it
with 1 tablespoon flour. Strain
the gravy and reserve the
onions. Stir the flour and fat
into the gravy and reboil. Set
aside.

Heat the chestnut purée, and
add the onions, season well
and add a nut of butter. Lay this
down the centre of a serving
dish, slice the venison and
arrange on the top. Spoon over
the gravy and garnish with
croquettes of celeriac.

To prepare the croquettes :
peel the celeriac and cut into
wedge-shape pieces, simmer in
salted water until barely tender.
Drain well, leave till cool and
then roll in seasoned flour,
brush with beaten egg, then
coat well with the crumbs. Fry
in butter until golden-brown.

Partridge with black olives

3 plumb partridges
1½ - 2 oz butter
4-6 oz green bacon rashers
3 shallots (finely chopped)
1 tablespoon plain flour
1 teaspoon tomato purée
½ pint well-flavoured, jellied stock
(see page 134)
2 wineglasses red wine
salt and pepper
bouquet garni
3 oz black olives (stoned and
halved)

Method

Set the oven at 325-350°F or
Mark 3-4. Brown the birds slowly
and carefully all over in the
butter in a flameproof casserole.
Meantime cut bacon into strips,
blanch and drain. Add these to
the pan with the shallots and
continue to fry gently for 3-4
minutes, then remove the birds ;
stir in the flour and add the
tomato purée and the stock.
Reduce the wine by about one-
third in a small saucepan and
add this to the casserole. Bring
to the boil. Season, add the
bouquet garni and replace the
partridges.

Cover with a piece of paper
or foil and then the lid. Cook in
the pre-set oven for 50-60
minutes, or until tender. Take
up partridges, remove trussing
strings, split in half and trim
away some backbone. Arrange
on a dish, boil the sauce rapidly
for 2-3 minutes, or until syrupy,
then add the black olives.
Reboil sauce and spoon it over
the dish at once.

Partridges

There are two varieties :
the English, or grey,
partridge and the French
partridge, also known as the
frenchman, which is slightly
larger than the English one
and has red legs. The
Frenchman is continental
in origin and is more
common than the English
bird, especially in the
eastern counties of England.

The English partridge is
especially prized for its
flavour when it is young.
The French partridge is
considered at its best when
more mature.

Partridges normande

2-3 partridges (according to size)
1½ oz clarified butter
2-3 shallots (finely chopped)
2 medium-size apples
  (preferably Cox's, or Pippin)
2 tablespoons Calvados (apple
  brandy)
7½ fl oz jellied stock (see page 134)
bouquet garni
salt and pepper
about ¼-½ oz kneaded butter
1 small carton (2½ fl oz) double
  cream
chopped parsley

Method

Heat a flameproof casserole, put in the butter, then the birds, breast-side downwards. Brown them slowly all over (this will take 7-10 minutes), then add the shallots and cook slowly, turning the birds every now and again, for a further 3 minutes. Quarter, core and slice the apples. Heat the Calvados, set it alight and pour flaming into the casserole. Add the stock, apples, the bouquet garni and seasoning. Bring to the boil and cook gently, either on top of the cooker or in the oven, pre-set at 325-350°F or Mark 3-4, for 45-50 minutes, or longer if the birds are not tender at the end of this time.

Watchpoint If the liquor in the pan evaporates too much, add a little extra stock during cooking.

Take up the partridges, remove the trussing strings and split each bird in half, trim away a little of the backbone with scissors and arrange on a serving dish. Turn the contents of casserole into a strainer, first removing the bouquet garni, and rub through. Return this liquid to the casserole, thicken very lightly with a little kneaded butter and, when boiling, add the cream. Boil hard for 1-2 minutes, then spoon sauce over the birds and sprinkle well with chopped parsley. Serve with château potatoes (see page 138).

Casserole of partridge
with braised red cabbage

3 French partridges
$\frac{1}{2}$-$\frac{3}{4}$ pint stock (made with carcasses, root vegetables and bouquet garni — see page 134)
1-1$\frac{1}{2}$ oz butter
$\frac{1}{4}$ lb chipolata sausages
1 onion (sliced)
1 carrot (sliced)
1 rasher of bacon (blanched and diced)
1 dessertspoon plain flour
bouquet garni
4-6 croûtes of fried bread
watercress (to garnish)

For stuffing
1 shallot (finely chopped)
1 oz butter
3 oz fresh white breadcrumbs
1$\frac{1}{2}$ oz raisins (stoned)
1 oz chopped walnuts
1 teaspoon finely chopped parsley
1 small egg (beaten)
salt and pepper

Trussing needle and fine string, or poultry pins

Casserole of partridge with red cabbage. The birds are served on croûtes

Method

Bone out the partridges (as for pheasant, see page 124), leaving the leg bones in, then spread out birds on your work surface. Clean the carcasses, break them up and use to make the stock, with root vegetables and bouquet garni to flavour. Strain off the required quantity of stock and set aside.

Set oven at 325°F or Mark 3.

To prepare the stuffing : soften shallot in the butter, then mix with the remaining stuffing ingredients, binding mixture with the beaten egg and seasoning to taste. Spread stuffing on the partridges and sew up with fine string or secure with poultry pins.

Heat butter in a flameproof casserole, put in the sausages to brown slowly. Take them out and brown the partridges ; add the onion, carrot and bacon. Cook for 2-3 minutes, then dust with flour, add bouquet garni and reserved stock. Cover casserole tightly and braise slowly for 45-60 minutes in the oven.

When birds are tender, remove them from the casserole. Split them in half and serve each half on a croûte of fried bread. Cut sausages in half diagonally and add to the casserole. Spoon a little of the sauce and the sausages over each croûte and serve the rest separately, together with braised red cabbage (see right). Garnish dish with watercress.

Braised red cabbage

1½-2 lb red cabbage
1 onion
1 oz butter
2 cooking apples
2-3 tablespoons wine vinegar
1 rounded tablespoon granulated
   sugar
salt and pepper
1 oz kneaded butter

Method

Wash and quarter the cabbage, cut out the stalk and shred finely. Put into a large pan of boiling water, cook 1 minute only, then drain well. (The cabbage will turn a deep violet at this point but when the vinegar is added later it returns to its original colour.)

Slice the onion and cook in the butter until soft but not coloured. Peel and slice the apples, add to the onion and continue cooking 2-3 minutes. Turn out on to a plate.

Add the cabbage to the pan, layering with the apple mixture and sprinkling with the vinegar, 2-3 tablespoons water, sugar and seasoning. Cover with buttered paper and lid and cook in a slow oven for 1½ - 2 hours at 325°F or Mark 3. Stir from time to time and moisten with a little extra water, or stock, if necessary.

When very tender stir in the kneaded butter a small piece at a time, adding enough to bind the cabbage and juices. Adjust the seasoning.

This cabbage is even better cooked the day before, and then reheated just before serving.

131

Partridge with cabbage (Perdrix au chou)

2 partridges
1 hard green cabbage (not a Savoy), weighing 2 lb after washing and trimming
salt and pepper
6 oz green streaky bacon (in the piece)
1 oz bacon fat, or butter
piece of fresh pork rind (about 6 inches by 4 inches)
2 medium-size carrots
4 oz pork sausages
1 large onion (stuck with a clove)
bouquet garni
1 pint stock (see page 134)
1 dessertspoon arrowroot (mixed with 1 tablespoon stock), or kneaded butter (made with 1 oz butter and 1 tablespoon flour)

Method

Set oven at 325°F or Mark 3.

Cut the cabbage in four, blanch it in boiling salted water, drain and refresh, then squeeze it gently in a clean cloth. Cut each quarter into 2-3 pieces and season lightly between the leaves. Drop the bacon in cold water, bring to the boil, drain and refresh.

Heat the bacon fat in a heavy flameproof casserole, brown the birds on all sides and then remove them from the pan. Put the piece of pork rind, fat side down, at the bottom of the casserole and cover with a layer of cabbage, about one-third of the total quantity. Replace the partridges, arrange the whole carrots, bacon, sausages, onion and bouquet garni on top. Put the remaining cabbage in the pan, moisten it with the stock and season. Cover with a buttered paper and tightly fitting lid and put in preset very moderate oven.

If the partridges are young

birds, remove them from the casserole after 35 minutes. If old, they can remain in with the cabbage, which must be cooked for at least $1\frac{1}{2}$ hours.

Take out the sausages after 35 minutes and the bacon after 45 minutes. Keep these ingredients covered to prevent them drying while the cabbage is completing its cooking time, but put them back again for 8-10 minutes before dishing up to make sure they are really hot.

To dish up, carve each partridge in four, cut the bacon in lardons and the sausages and carrots in rounds. Drain the cabbage in a colander over a saucepan, remove the onion and pork rind and then press the cabbage lightly to remove all the liquid. Place the cabbage in the serving dish, arrange the partridge on top and the bacon, sausage and carrot round the edge ; keep warm. Thicken the strained juices with the slaked arrowroot or kneaded butter, taste for seasoning. Spoon a little of this sauce round the cabbage and serve the rest in a sauce boat.

Appendix

Stocks

As every good cook knows, the best casseroles, stews, braises and sauces owe their fine flavour to the original stock. Poor stock can turn a promising dish into a dull and tasteless mixture. If a recipe calls for good stock and you don't have any to hand (nor feel like making some), then change your choice of dish. Trying to compromise can lead to failure in making a special dish.

Stock is easy to make once you know how, and its ingredients are not expensive. Most larders have something — vegetables, carcass bones and so on — which can be turned into a small quantity of stock for a gravy or a simple sauce. If you want more, a few beef bones from the butcher will make enough stock for a week for the average family needs. Bones, on their own, will make a stronger stock than if you use mixed vegetables and bits of meat (mixed stock).

Raw mutton bones and turnips are best left out of stocks unless you are making a Scotch broth ; both have a strong flavour and could well spoil the dish for which the stock is intended.

The liquid in a stockpot should be reduced in quantity (by simmering) by about a quarter, or even more, before the stock is ready for straining.

In an emergency a **bouillon cube** can be used for certain things, but it can never replace properly-made stock because it will lack the characteristic jellied quality. Bouillon cubes are salty and there is always the danger of overdoing the seasoning. If you use cubes too often as the basis of your stock, your dishes will not only have a monotonous flavour but the bouillon cube taste will give you away.

Mixed stock

If you want a really clear stock, the only way to make it is to use raw bones. If you are using cooked ones as well, it helps to add them after the stock has come to the boil, although it is better not to mix raw with cooked bones if the stock is to be kept for any length of time.

Any trimmings or leftovers in the way of meat can go into your regular stockpot : chicken carcasses and giblets (but not the liver) ; bacon rinds ; or a ham or bacon bone. This last is often given away and it makes excellent stock for a pea soup.

Add a plateful of cut-up root vegetables, a bouquet garni, 5-6 peppercorns, and pour in enough cold water to cover the ingredients by two-thirds. Salt very lightly, or not at all if there is a bacon bone in the pot. Bring slowly to the boil, skim, half-cover the pan and simmer $1\frac{1}{2}$-2 hours or longer, depending on the quantity of stock being made. The liquid should reduce by about a third. Strain off and, when the stock is cold, skim well to remove any fat. Throw away the ingredients unless a fair amount of raw bones have been used, in which case more water can be added and a second boiling made.

If the stock is to be kept several days, or if there is a fair proportion of chicken in it, bring to the boil every day. If you are keeping it in the refrigerator, save room by storing, covered, in a jug instead of a bowl. Remember that the stronger the stock, the better it will keep.

Watchpoint Long slow simmering is essential for any meat stock. It should never be allowed to boil hard as this will result in a thick muddy-looking jelly instead of a semi-clear one.

Brown bone stock

3 lb beef bones (or mixed beef/veal)
2 onions (quartered)
2 carrots (quartered)
1 stick of celery (sliced)
large bouquet garni
6 peppercorns
3-4 quarts water
salt

6-quart capacity saucepan, or small fish kettle

Method
Wipe bones but do not wash unless unavoidable. Put into a very large pan. Set on gentle heat and leave bones to fry gently for 15-20 minutes. Enough fat will come out from the marrow so do not add any to pan unless bones are very dry. After 10 minutes add the vegetables.

When bones and vegetables are just coloured, add herbs, peppercorns and the water, which should come up two-thirds above level of ingredients. Bring slowly to the boil, skimming occasionally, then half cover pan and simmer 4-5 hours, or until stock tastes strong and good.

Strain off and use bones again for a second boiling. Although this second stock will not be so strong as the first, it is good for soups and gravies. Use the first stock for brown sauces, sautés, casseroles, or where a **jellied stock** is required. For a strong beef broth, add 1 lb shin of beef to the pot halfway through the cooking.

White bone stock

This stock forms a basis for cream sauces, white stews, etc. It is made in the same way as brown bone stock, except that bones and vegetables are not browned before the water is added, and veal bones are used. Do not add the vegetables until the bones have come to the boil and fat has been skimmed off.

Vegetable stock

1 lb carrots
1 lb onions
$\frac{1}{2}$ head of celery
$\frac{1}{2}$ oz butter
3-4 peppercorns
1 teaspoon tomato purée
2 quarts water
salt

Method
Quarter vegetables, brown lightly in the butter in a large pan. Add peppercorns, tomato purée, water and salt. Bring to boil, cover pan and simmer 2 hours or until the stock has a good flavour.

Chicken stock

This should ideally be made from the giblets (neck, gizzard, heart and feet, if available), but never the liver which imparts a bitter flavour. This is better kept for making pâté, or sautéd and used as a savoury. Dry fry the giblets with an onion, washed but not peeled, and cut in half. To dry fry, use a thick pan with a lid, with barely enough fat to cover the bottom. Allow the pan to get very hot before putting in the giblets and onion, cook on full heat until lightly coloured. Remove pan from heat before covering with 2 pints of cold water. Add a large pinch of salt, a few peppercorns and a bouquet garni (bayleaf, thyme, parsley) and simmer gently for 1-2 hours. Alternatively, make the stock when you cook the chicken by putting the giblets in the roasting tin around the chicken with the onion and herbs, and use the measured quantity of water.

Notes and basic recipes

Béchamel sauce

$\frac{3}{4}$ pint milk
slice of onion
6 peppercorns
1 blade of mace
1 bayleaf
1 tablespoon cream (optional)

For roux

1 oz butter
2 tablespoons plain flour
salt and pepper

Method

Infuse milk with onion and spices in a covered pan over a low heat for 5-7 minutes, but do not boil. Pour the milk into a basin and wipe the pan out.

To make the roux: melt the butter slowly, remove pan from heat and stir in the flour. Pour on at least one-third of the milk through a strainer and blend together with a wooden spoon. Then add the rest of the milk, season lightly, return to heat and stir until boiling. Boil for not more than 2 minutes, then taste for seasoning. The sauce may be finished with 1 tablespoon of cream.

Breadcrumbs

To make white crumbs: take a large loaf (the best type is a sandwich loaf) at least two days old. Cut off the crust and keep to one side. Break up bread into crumbs either by rubbing through a wire sieve or a Mouli sieve, or by working in an electric blender.

Spread crumbs on to a sheet of paper laid on a baking tin and cover with another sheet of paper to keep off any dust. Leave to dry in a warm temperature — the plate rack, or warming drawer, or the top of the oven, or even the airing cupboard, is ideal. The crumbs may take a day or two to dry thoroughly, and they must be crisp before storing. To make them uniformly fine sift them through a wire bowl strainer.

To make browned crumbs: bake the crusts in a slow oven until golden-brown, then crush or grind through a mincer. Sift crumbs through a wire bocol strainer to make them uniformally fine. Store all crumbs in a dry, screw-top jar.

Carrots
Carrots (glazed)

1-2 lb carrots
1 teaspoon sugar
1 oz butter
salt
mint (chopped)

Method

Peel carrots and leave whole, or quarter if small. If very large, cut in thin slices. Put in a pan with water to cover, sugar, butter and a pinch of salt. Cover and cook steadily until tender, then remove lid and cook until all the water has evaporated, when the butter and sugar will form a glaze round the carrots.

Add a little chopped mint just before serving.

Carrots in poulette sauce

1 lb large carrots
$\frac{1}{2}$ oz butter
1 teaspoon sugar

For 'quick' poulette sauce

1 oz butter
1 rounded tablespoon plain flour
$\frac{3}{4}$ cup of vegetable, or chicken, stock
salt and pepper
5 tablespoons top of the milk
$\frac{1}{2}$ teaspoon lemon juice
1 large teaspoon chopped parsley

Method

Peel the carrots, cut them into thin rounds and put in a saucepan with the butter and sugar and cold water to cover. Cook them, covered, until tender (15-20 minutes).

To prepare poulette sauce : melt the butter, stir in the flour and cook over a low heat until a pale straw-colour. Draw pan aside, pour on the stock and blend until smooth. Return pan to the heat and stir until mixture begins to thicken, then season and add milk. Bring sauce to the boil and cook another 2-3 minutes until syrupy in consistency. Draw pan aside and add the lemon juice and parsley.

Remove the lid from the pan of carrots, boil rapidly until all the water is driven off and the carrots are coated in a glaze of butter and sugar. Pour the sauce over the carrots and serve.

Forcemeat balls

1 cup fresh white breadcrumbs
1 oz suet
salt and pepper
2 tablespoons chopped
  mixed herbs and parsley
1 small egg (beaten)

Method
Mix the crumbs and suet together, season well, add herbs and bind with the beaten egg. Roll this mixture into small balls and use as required.

Onions (glazed)

Cover the onions with cold water, add salt and bring to the boil. Tip off the water, add 1-1 $\frac{1}{2}$ oz butter and a dusting of caster sugar. Cover and cook gently until golden-brown on all sides, and cooked through (about 10 minutes).

Pistachio nuts

To blanch nuts, pour boiling water over and add a pinch of bicarbo-

nate of soda to preserve colour. Cover pan and leave until cool. Then skins can be easily removed with fingers.

Polenta balls

5 tablespoons polenta (maize meal)
$\frac{1}{2}$-$\frac{3}{4}$ pint water
$\frac{1}{2}$ oz butter
1 egg
1 tablespoon grated cheese
salt and pepper
French mustard

For crumbing

1 beaten egg
dry white breadcrumbs

Deep fat (for frying)

Method
Bring the water to the boil, sift in the polenta and simmer for 7 minutes, stirring frequently. Take off the heat and beat in the butter, egg and cheese, then season well with salt, pepper and mustard. Spread on a plate to cool. Shape into small balls on a floured board, brush with beaten egg and roll in breadcrumbs. Fry in deep fat until golden-brown.

Potatoes
Boulangère potatoes

1 $\frac{1}{2}$ lb potatoes (thinly sliced)
3 medium-size onions
salt and pepper
$\frac{3}{4}$ pint stock
1 bayleaf
1 tablespoon dripping

Method
Slice onions, blanch by putting in cold water, bringing to the boil and boiling for 1 minute before draining. Peel and slice potatoes in thin rounds and place immediately in an ovenproof dish layered with the onions, salt and pepper. Pour over just enough stock to cover and add bayleaf.

Dot well with dripping and bake for 1 hour in an oven at 400°F or Mark 6 until tender and well browned.

To get the best results, remove from oven halfway through cooking time when, if top layer of potatoes has curled up, press down into the stock with basting spoon and add a little extra dripping, if necessary.

Chateau potatoes

1 lb old, or new, potatoes
1-2 oz butter
salt

Method

Old potatoes should be blanched before browning. Cut peeled potatoes into quarters lengthways, then use a potato peeler to trim off sharp edges (blanch, drain and dry). If using new potatoes, scrape and leave them whole, wash and dry them thoroughly, but do not blanch.

Melt butter in a casserole, add potatoes and cook over a moderate heat until golden-brown, shaking casserole occasionally to stop them from sticking. Season lightly, cover and put into oven to finish cooking for 10-12 minutes at 400°F or Mark 6.

Dauphinois potatoes

1 lb potatoes (weight when peeled)
$\frac{1}{2}$-$\frac{3}{4}$ oz butter
1 clove of garlic
salt and pepper
small pinch of nutmeg
1$\frac{1}{4}$ oz grated cheese
1 egg
good $\frac{1}{2}$ pint milk

8 $\frac{1}{2}$ -9 inch long shallow ovenproof dish

Method

Set oven at 350-375°F or Mark 4-5, and well butter the dish.

Crush the garlic with a pinch of

salt and work it into the rest of the butter. Spread this on the bottom and sides of the dish, then slice the potatoes thinly and arrange them neatly in the dish. Season well, add the pinch of nutmeg, and sprinkle with 1 oz of the cheese. Beat the egg with a fork ; scald the milk and pour it on to the egg. Then pour this mixture in at the side of the dish. Scatter over the rest of the cheese, set the dish in a roasting tin of hot water and bake in pre-set moderately hot oven, on the top shelf, for 45-50 minutes. Serve hot in the dish.

Fondant potatoes

2-2 $\frac{1}{2}$ lb small new potatoes
1 $\frac{1}{2}$-2 oz butter
salt

Method

Scrape the potatoes, rinse well in cold water and dry in a tea towel. Melt the butter in a sauté pan, add the potatoes, cover and set over a very moderate heat. Shake the pan from time to time to turn the potatoes, but do not lift the lid for the first 10-15 minutes as the steam not only helps the potatoes to cook more quickly, but also prevents sticking. Test to see if the potatoes are tender, season with salt and turn on to a hot serving dish.

Maître d'hôtel potatoes

1 $\frac{1}{2}$ lb even-size potatoes
1 $\frac{1}{2}$ oz butter
1 shallot (chopped)
2 tablespoons chopped parsley
salt and pepper

Method

Scrub potatoes and boil or steam in their skins until tender but firm. Drain and dry. Peel potatoes, slice and arrange in a hot dish and keep warm.

Melt butter in a small pan, add

shallot, cover pan and set on low heat for 2-3 minutes. Then draw aside, add parsley and plenty of seasoning and pour over the potatoes. Slide into the oven for 2-3 minutes before serving.

Sauté potatoes

1½ lb potatoes
2 tablespoons oil
1 oz butter
salt and pepper
1 dessertspoon chopped parsley

Method
Scrub potatoes and boil in their skins until very tender. Then drain, peel and slice. After heating a frying pan, put in oil and when this is hot add the butter. Slip in all the potatoes at once, add seasoning and cook (sauté) until golden-brown and crisp, yet buttery, occasionally turning the contents of the pan. Draw aside, check seasoning, and add parsley. Serve in a very hot dish.

Redcurrant jelly

It is not possible to give a specific quantity of redcurrants as the recipe is governed by the amount of juice made, which is variable.

Method
Wash the fruit and, without removing from the stems, put in a 7 lb jam jar or stone crock. Cover and stand in deep pan of hot water. Simmer on top of the stove or in the oven at 350°F or Mark 4, mashing the fruit a little from time to time, until all the juice is extracted (about 1 hour).

Then turn fruit into a jelly-bag, or double linen strainer, and allow to drain undisturbed overnight over a basin.

Watchpoint To keep the jelly clear and sparkling, do not try to speed up the draining process by forcing juice through ; this will only make the jelly cloudy.

Now measure juice. Allowing 1 lb lump or preserving sugar to each pint of juice, mix juice and sugar together, dissolving over slow heat. When dissolved, bring to the boil, boil hard for 3-5 minutes and skim with a wooden spoon. Test a little on a saucer : allow jelly to cool, tilt saucer and, if jelly is set, it will wrinkle. Put into jam jars, place small circles of grease-proof paper over jelly, label and cover with jam pot covers. Store in a dry larder until required.

Rice

Most people have their own favourite method of boiling rice. That recommended by Asians is to cook the rice in a small quantity of boiling water until this is absorbed, when rice is soft. The amount of water varies according to the quality of the rice. This method is good but can present problems. Really the simplest way is to cook the rice (about 2 oz washed rice per person) in plenty of boiling, well-salted water (3 quarts per 8 oz rice) for about 12 minutes. You can add a slice of lemon for flavour. Stir with a fork to prevent rice sticking while boiling, and watch that it does not overcook.

To stop rice cooking, either tip it quickly into a colander and drain, or pour ½ cup cold water into the pan and then drain. Pour over a jug of hot water to wash away the remaining starch, making several holes through the rice with the handle of a wooden spoon to help it drain more quickly.

To reheat : spoon into a buttered ovenproof dish, cover with buttered paper, put in oven at 350°F or Mark 4 for 30 minutes.

With a pilaf, the rice is cooked in stock until it has been absorbed and the rice is dry and flaky. Though this can be done over a flame, it is best to put the pan or casserole in the oven to get both top and bottom heat.

Spinach creams

(see photograph on page 60)

2 lb spinach
$\frac{1}{2}$ oz butter
béchamel sauce (made with 1 oz
    butter 1 oz plain flour and $\frac{1}{2}$ pint
    flavoured milk) — see page 136
2 eggs
salt and pepper
grate of nutmeg

8 dariole moulds

Method

Cook the spinach in a large pan of boiling salted water for 7 minutes ; drain, refresh and press between two plates to remove the excess water. In this way the delicate leaves remain whole and unbroken. Carefully lift 8 spinach leaves (16 if they are small) and use to line the buttered moulds ; sieve the remaining leaves.

Melt the butter, cook slowly to a nutbrown, add the spinach purée and stir over the heat until dry. Add the béchamel sauce and mix well. Draw aside. Beat in the eggs, season well with salt and pepper and a tiny grate of nutmeg.

Spoon the mixture into the prepared moulds, cover with buttered paper or foil and cook au bain-marie in the oven, under the tongues, at 350°F or Mark 4 for 15-20 minutes.

Tomatoes

To skin tomatoes : place them in a bowl, scald by pouring boiling water over them, count 12, then pour off the hot water and replace it with cold. The skin then comes off easily.

To remove seeds : slice off the top of each tomato and flick out seeds with the handle of a teaspoon, using the bowl of the spoon to detach the core.

Glossary

Bain-marie (au) To cook at temperature just below boiling point in a bain-marie (a saucepan standing in a larger pan of simmering water). May be carried out on top of stove or in oven.

Bard To cover lean meats / game with larding bacon / pork fat before cooking. See also **Lardons.**

Blanch To whiten meats and remove strong tastes from vegetables by bringing to boil from cold water and draining before further cooking. Green vegetables should be put into boiling water and cooked for up to 1 minute.

Bouquet garni Traditionally a bunch of parsley, thyme, bayleaf, for flavouring stews and sauces. Other herbs can be added. Remove before serving dish.

Butter, clarified Butter clarified by heating gently until foaming, skimming well, pouring off clear yellow oil, leaving sediment (milk solids) behind.

Butter, kneaded A liaison for thickening. Twice as much butter as flour is worked into a paste on a plate with a fork, and added in small pieces to the cooled mixture off the heat. Butter melts and draws flour into the liquid.

Croûte Small round of bread, lightly toasted or fried, spread or piled up with a savoury mixture, also used as a garnish. Not to be confused with pie or bread crust (also croûte).

Deglaze To heat stock and / or wine together with flavoursome sediments left in roasting / frying pan so that gravy / sauce is formed. (Remove excess fat first.)

Infuse To steep in liquid (not always boiling) in warm place to draw flavour into the liquid.

Lardons Small $\frac{1}{4}$-inch thick strips of fat about $1\frac{1}{2}$ inches long, cut from piece of larding bacon which is solid fat. They are used to give extra fat to cuts of meat that have little or none of their own to protect them from drying out during cooking. These strips are larded, or sewn, into the meat with a larding needle.

Liaison Mixture for thickening / binding sauce / gravy / soup eg. roux, egg yolks, cream kneaded butter.

Marinate To soak raw meat / game / fish in cooked or raw spiced liquid (marinade) of wine, oil, herbs and vegetables for hours / days before cooking. This softens, tenderises and flavours and a marinade can be used for the final sauce. Use glass / glazed / enamel / stainless steel vessel to withstand the effects of acid.

Parboil To boil until half-cooked.

Reduce To boil down sauce, or any liquid, to concentrate flavour and thicken the consistency.

Roux Fat and flour liaison. This is the basis of all flour sauces. The weight of fat should generally be slightly more than that of flour. To make, melt fat, stir in flour (off heat) and pour on water / stock / milk. Stir until roux thickens, bring to boil and cook.

Rust Underside of bacon rasher or ham, on the side opposite to the rind. It is often tough and strong flavoured, so should be cut off.

Sauté To brown food in butter, or oil and butter. Sometimes cooking is completed in a 'small' sauce — ie. one made on the food in the sauté pan.

Scald 1 To plunge into boiling water for easy peeling. **2** To heat a liquid, e.g. milk, to just under boiling point.

Seasoned flour Flour to which salt and pepper have been added.

Slake To mix arrowroot / cornflour with a little cold water before adding to a liquid for thickening.

Sweat To draw out flavour by cooking diced or sliced vegetables gently in a little melted butter in covered pan until softened (5-10 minutes).

Tammy strainer Strainer made of very fine double-mesh wire. When sauce is strained through this, it becomes very smooth and acquires a high gloss as a result of emulsification.

Index

143

144